# TOM PATTY'S

# MARKETING WITHOUT MONEY

by

## Tom Patty with Donna Jost

Book Cover Design by Susan Rinek

Endless Dreams Publishing

*Tom Patty's Marketing Without Money*

Published in the United States of America by

Endless Dreams Publishing
Dana Point CA  92629
info@endlessdreamspublishing.com
www.endlessdreamspublishing.com

Book Cover Designed by:
Susan Rinek
dsign46 Demographic
Newport Beach, CA

Library of Congress Control Number:
2013931713

ISBN 978-0-9852588-0-1

*"If I had more time, I'd make it shorter."*

—*Mark Twain*

# CONTENTS

# FOREWARD

From our first meeting, I could tell that Tom was different from other ad agency account managers with whom I had worked. His passion and extraordinary instincts for marketing were evident, and I knew pretty quickly that this guy really loved thinking about ideas that could help our business grow.

As Director of Advertising for Yamaha Motorcycles and Tom Patty's first major client when he started his career at Chiat/Day Advertising in 1977, I appreciated that Tom spoke his mind frankly and that he was committed to doing what was right for the client, even over conflicting needs of the agency that employed him. So you can imagine how this behavior allowed him to create very strong relationships with top executives at Yamaha, and his other clients.

My collaboration with Tom and his outstanding creative team at the agency (including advertising legend, Lee Clow) was mutually rewarding. Yamaha's business flourished and the agency's brilliant advertising shook up the industry, attracting new clients to the then small regional agency.

My career connected again with Tom when I joined Nissan Motor Corp., USA, in 1988 as Director of Advertising—a year after Chiat/Day won their national account in a competitive shoot-out.

While Nissan's resources were considerable, we were outspent in the market by all of our major competition. To maximize Nissan's sales, our marketing communications needed to be superior to the competition. If our efforts were twice as effective, we could, in effect, double our budget. Sometimes it's better to have a sharper nail than a bigger hammer.

When Tom asked me to read his manuscript, I was reminded of how he has always been able to make complex things seem easy to understand. He always used to say, "I want to be able to talk about marketing in a way that a five-year-old could understand."

Many business and marketing books can be dull and abstract and try to make marketing more complicated than necessary. In *Tom Patty's Marketing Without Money*, he has reduced all of the complexity and abstraction of marketing into a few relatively simple and specific strategies and ideas that anyone can understand and implement in his or her business.

Now that Tom has retired from the advertising business and joined SCORE, volunteering his time and expertise to help small-business owners and entrepreneurs, I am not surprised that his marketing seminars are highly attended, and that his one-on-one counseling sessions are fully booked months in advance. As Tom would say, if you love what you do, success will follow.

*Tom Patty's Marketing Without Money* very clearly, simply and entertainingly presents a highly useful guide to the marketing process. Readers who embrace the marketing passion and insights in this book can grow their businesses beyond their wildest dreams.

*John Rinek,*
*Past Director of Marketing Communications,*
*Nissan North America, Inc.*

# LETTER TO THE READER

## *My Failed Experience as an Entrepreneur*

In 1998, at the age of 53, I retired as President, World Wide Account Director of the L.A. office of TBWA Chiat/Day Advertising Agency.

I had spent 21 years at this agency and helped grow the annual revenues from about $30 million to more than $100 million. Our advertising agency worked on some of the most prestigious and biggest brands in the marketing world, including Apple, Pizza Hut, Nike, Nissan, Infiniti, and Yamaha Motorcycles. I worked personally with top executives—CEOs and Marketing Directors—at most of these companies.

Once I retired from the advertising business, after a few months of traveling and goofing off, I decided to start my own company in March 1999. I had gotten back into music—something I always loved—and created a CD featuring 10 songs that I wrote, sang, and produced with the help of my producer, Jeffrey Foskett, who worked with the Beach Boys. The CD was entitled, "Living on the Island Side of Life" and I positioned myself as the "Jimmy Buffett of the West."

My goal was to sell my CD on Amazon.com, using it as the beginning of a whole array of products to help my target audience—Baby Boomers—prepare for retirement.

Seriously, how hard could it be to sell a few thousand CDs on the Internet? I was a marketing guru who had given advice to CEOs of some of the most successful companies in America. I figured this would be a piece of cake.

Unfortunately, I found out very quickly and quite painfully I might add, that my idea was a lot more difficult than I had imagined. I also learned the following very important realities:

• It's a lot easier to create a product than to sell it.

• The Internet is simply another distribution system, not a magic bullet for marketing success.

• When I worked at the agency, I had a big staff that helped me get things done. Now, I was on my own.

• It is very difficult to spend your time working only on productive and necessary tasks to get a business off the ground, and not get sucked into the less-important fun "stuff."

As a result, I made a lot of mistakes, of which a longer list follows:

• I did not understand how many CDs I would have to sell to break even.

• I wasn't aware that people weren't willing to pay for music because they could download it for free.

• I wasted money hiring a PR firm to do things I could easily have done myself.

• I also spent too much time and energy on things that really didn't matter; i.e., business cards, stationary, etc.

• I didn't understand the necessity of creating an experience by performing live in local venues.

• I had no idea as to who my target audience was, (i.e., not Baby Boomers.)

I could go on and on, but you get the idea. My business was a failure, my biggest problem being that I couldn't find enough people who loved my music. Hence, I was unable to generate sufficient sales to break even.·

Fortunately, I didn't need this business to succeed. I had retired with enough money to provide a very comfortable lifestyle. However, I really enjoyed the process of creating the CD. So, even though the business was a failure, the experience was very positive and I was happy I did it.

What emerged from this experience, though, was a newfound respect and admiration for anyone who has the courage and determination to start a business. I now know how difficult and overwhelming it is to create something out of nothing. Feeling a kinship with people who wanted to take a risk, especially in this economic climate, I decided to put my expertise to good use and write this book, *Tom Patty's Marketing Without Money.*

## DO NOT JUST READ THIS BOOK

Most books are designed to be read, enjoyed, studied, then put on the shelf to collect dust, but not *Marketing Without Money.* Please do not just read this book. I want you to USE it as a working tool to help you understand the concept of marketing. Think of it as a map to navigate your course from a small, struggling business to a thriving, growing enterprise with lots of customers who love and appreciate you and your products and services.

In *Marketing Without Money*, I have tried to make the subject of marketing easy to understand by giving you specific recommendations about how you can apply these principles to help grow your business. I promise that if you follow my suggestions, you can become a better marketer and, as a result, more successful.

# PREFACE

## *It Starts With Why*

One of the best business books published in the last few years, that I recommend to people in my marketing seminars, is entitled, *Start With Why: How Great Leaders Inspire Everyone To Take Action*, by Simon Sinek. According to Sinek, the basic premise of the book is: "People don't buy what you do; they buy why you do it."[1]

In the two examples below, Sinek provides a comparison between the usual way that people try to sell a computer, followed by Apple's approach.

**Normal Sales Pitch:** "We make great computers. They're beautifully designed, simple to use, and user-friendly. Wanna buy one?" [2]

**Apple's Pitch:** "Everything we do, we believe in challenging the status quo. We believe in thinking differently. The way we challenge the status quo is by making our products beautifully designed, simple to use and user-friendly. We just happen to make great computers. Want to buy one?" [3]

What I learned from these two examples is that I should explain to you why I wanted to write this book. What is my purpose? What is my "why?"

1 Simon Sinek, "Start With Why: How Great Leaders Inspire Everyone To Take Action" (Portfolio Trade 2011) Page 41
2 Sinek Page 40
3 Sinek Page 41

The first thing you need to understand is that writing a book is not much fun. I have written a couple of books before (30 years ago) and I knew it would be a difficult and demanding project. As Winston Churchill so eloquently put it, "Writing a book is an adventure. To begin with, it is a toy and an amusement. Then it becomes a mistress, then it becomes a master, then it becomes a tyrant. The last phase is that just as you are about to be reconciled to your servitude, you kill the monster and fling him to the public."[4]

*Marketing Without Money* basically grew out of my 21-year career in the advertising business, but much more of the book came from 10 years as a volunteer for SCORE, a national non-profit organization that provides free counseling and other resources to small-business owners around the country. SCORE recruits successful business executives in all areas—finance, manufacturing, marketing, etc.—who volunteer their time, expertise, and knowledge to help entrepreneurs grow their business.

I joined the Orange County, California, Chapter of SCORE in 2002 and over the past decade I have given marketing seminars and workshops around Southern California to thousands of small-business owners.

Sitting down face-to-face for counseling sessions with some of my seminar attendees, I am constantly reminded how hard it is to start a business from scratch. These people are so understaffed, undercapitalized, and overworked that they don't want to hear philosophical abstractions and platitudes about marketing. They want simple, straight talk. They want specific and concrete ideas that they can use to increase their revenues, to sell more products or services.

---

4  Winston Churchill quotes (British Orator, Author and Prime Minister during World War II. 1874-1965)

These small-business owners are so very different from my clients at the advertising agency. Unlike Apple, Nissan, Nike, Pizza Hut, etc., these small-business owners do not have large multi-million dollar advertising or marketing budgets. In fact, most of them do not have a budget at all.

Another huge difference is that they are not financially able to hire a large staff to get things done. No 20-person marketing department, no outside advertising agency; generally it is just one, two, maybe three people who have to handle everything.

Over the years I have developed a way of communicating with these people. I understand their needs and realities, and in many cases I am able to help them grow their businesses. A few of my SCORE clients have even gone on to achieve spectacular success, doubling, and in some instances, tripling and quadrupling their business.

You might ask, what's in it for me, Tom Patty? Why do I spend so much time with my SCORE clients when I could be out sailing my boat or riding my bike? The truth of the matter is that I get great satisfaction from watching and, in some small way, participating in the success of my SCORE clients. I don't do it for the money; there's absolutely no financial remuneration for me. I do it for the love. So, let's get down to business.

## Who Is My Target Audience for This Book?

My target audience for *Marketing Without Money* consists of entrepreneurs and owners of small and mid-size businesses who are willing to ask for help, are receptive to the idea that they may have to change their approach to business, really want to increase their revenues, and are prepared to do the hard work required to be successful.

I'm not going to lie to you. I do not pretend to have a magic bullet or a quick solution that will suddenly catapult your business into success. This is not instant coffee; it's not fast food, nor is it marketing without effort and brains.

## What Benefits Can You Expect?

My distinctive competitive advantage is that I have over two decades of big-league marketing experience with famous brands such as Apple, Nike, Pizza Hut, Nissan, and Chiat/Day Advertising, combined with 10 years of one-on-one personal counseling through SCORE with small-business owners and entrepreneurs just like you. As a result, I can provide you with an overview of the marketing world and specific blueprints for action that you can use to increase your sales and revenues.

## QR Codes

In various chapters of this book you will see a small square box similar to a bar code, but with a squiggly graphic inside. Randomly placed, but relative to what you are reading, these graphics or QR Codes allow your smartphone to scan the code to connect with my YouTube, *Marketing Without Money* video clips from my SCORE seminars. Although QR Codes are somewhat unfamiliar in the literary world, they will hopefully add another entertaining and interesting dimension to this book.

## What Do I Need From You?

What I need from you is patience and trust that I will be a good teacher. I know you want quick and easy solutions. You don't want to know how the watch is made. You just want to know what time it is. But it has been my experience that small-business owners need to understand the basics of marketing before they attempt to use the tools.

A good example is learning to play the guitar. I started playing when I was in my twenties. I was impatient. I did not want to learn the fundamentals of music theory. I just wanted to know a few chords so I could play a handful of songs. Because I didn't learn the basic elements, I never became an accomplished musician on the guitar, and even after 40 years, I am still not able to fully utilize the instrument.

While it has taken me more than 30 years to accumulate my understanding of marketing, I surely don't expect you to wait that long to become proficient. However, the better you understand the fundamentals, the more effective and successful you will be as a marketer.

## How This Book is Organized

*Marketing Without Money* is organized around answering two fundamental questions:

- WHAT is marketing?
- HOW can you use marketing to grow your business?

Chapters 1 through 5 in the book deal primarily with the "WHAT" of marketing, explaining the basic concepts. The rest of the book delves into "HOW" you can apply these marketing concepts to your business.

So, in the next 16 chapters, I ask you to have faith that I will tell you very specifically what you need to do and how to do it. Trust, people, trust.

# MARKETING
# IS TO BUSINESS
# WHAT SEX IS TO PEOPLE

# Chapter 1

# MARKETING IS TO BUSINESS WHAT SEX IS TO PEOPLE

Trust me…In my seminars, I like to say that marketing is as essential to business as sex is to human life. If you think about it, there are a number of similarities between the two. First, like sex, marketing is an activity, not some intellectual construct. Second, sex and marketing should each be fun and exciting. And finally, the primary requirement for both is to make oneself or one's product/service attractive to someone else. In the same way that peacocks have developed elaborate colorful tails to attract the opposite sex, your business must figure out how to make your products or services irresistible to your customers and clients.

At least from a biological perspective, the objective of sex is to propagate the species. No sex, no species. The same is true in business. Without successful marketing, your business cannot survive from one generation to the next. From the same biological standpoint, the goal of sex is to transmit your DNA to live on. In marketing, you must pass on ideas about your brand to the consumer.

In life, whenever you want a long-term relationship with another human being, you look for certain attributes. You want someone who is trustworthy, dependable, honest, and unselfish. Ironically, these are the same traits that your customers will look for in your business, which, if successful, will create a positive relationship between a business and a customer.

Lastly, marketing, like sex, is about fulfilling needs and wants. A business that figures out how to satisfy more customers will be more successful than those that don't pay attention to consumers' desires.

I honestly believe that every small-business owner and entrepreneur engages in marketing to some extent. If you have a product or service, and a customer, by my definition you are marketing. You may not be doing it well or efficiently, or even effectively for that matter, but you are still marketing.

In the next few chapters, I will give you specific ways to attract more customers by thinking about 1) how people see your product or service, 2) how you can make it more accessible, 3) how it can be perceived as a better value, and 4) how to get more exposure.

# PART I:
# WHAT?

# WHAT DOES "MARKETING WITHOUT MONEY" REALLY MEAN?

*Marketing is About Ideas*

.

## Chapter 2

# WHAT DOES "MARKETING WITHOUT MONEY" REALLY MEAN?

### *Marketing is About Ideas*

*Marketing Without Money* means that you can be a very successful marketer without a large marketing or advertising budget. You just need to substitute creative ideas for money.

I personally believe that anyone can be creative. You don't need a degree. You don't need to be Einstein. You just have to be able to look at something in a new and fresh way; have a unique perspective. It may cost money to implement it, but the idea itself is free.

The following are examples of great marketing campaigns that stimulated business growth and started with just an idea.

**PIZZA HUT: Deliver Fresh Pizza to Homes**

I worked on the Pizza Hut account at Chiat/Day from 1983 to 1985 with Steve Reinemund, President/CEO of Pizza Hut, who eventually went on to become the CEO of their multi-billion-dollar parent company, PepsiCo, Inc.

In 1985, Pizza Hut had more than 1,000 restaurants across the country, mainly franchised operations that served people in the restaurant, as well as take-out. But they had no delivery business. That was dominated by the newcomer, Domino's. One day, Steve Reinemund called me up and said they wanted to create a delivery business for the Pizza Hut stores.

We quickly discovered that launching a new method of distribution, namely delivery, was much more complicated than anyone expected. But within two years, their delivery business was contributing a substantial increase in sales to Pizza Hut.

It started with an idea, a simple question: "How can we make it easier and more convenient for our customers to get and consume our product?" In this case, the answer was "delivery."

## U.S. POST OFFICE: "If It Fits, It Ships"

Even the U.S. Post Office can be creative! They came up with a way to take the mystery and complexity out of the cost of shipping packages. It's such a simple concept: three sizes of boxes, each with a different price. No more time taken up weighing packages on the postal scales; if your items fit in the box, you know what it will cost. The execution, a way to convey benefits, was as brilliant and simple as its slogan: "If it fits, it ships."

## THE APPLE STORE

For many years, Apple's primary distribution system depended upon dealers and big-box retailers like Best Buy. Then one day they announced that they were launching "The Apple Store." The idea was to own and operate retail stores in selected locations around the country.

This was not a new idea. Gateway Computers tried it and failed back in the 90s. Remember the black and white boxes that were supposed to look like cows? Even the experts agreed that it was a terrible idea for Apple to attempt. This is a great example, however, that proves that just because something failed doesn't necessarily mean it's a bad idea. You always have to ask yourself the question: "Was the idea bad or was the specific execution bad?"

Apple ended up succeeding because 1) their stores were better with a more interesting design and layout, 2) their brand was stronger, 3) the locations of the stores were more thought-out, and 4) Steve Jobs was a better marketer than the founder and CEO of Gateway.

Proving to be a really big marketing idea for Apple, this helped propel them into a whole new league. Apple is no longer just a manufacturer; they are now a retailer, which gives customers a way to physically connect with the brand in the same way that church allows people to connect with their religion.

## SOUTHWEST AIRLINES: "Bags Fly Free"

The great marketing of the brilliant television campaign for Southwest Airlines, "Bags Fly Free", isn't the commercial, which, by the way, is excellent. It's the concept, the idea. This marketing idea works because it positions Southwest Airlines against the competition's practice of charging for bags, leaving them looking like the good guy while making fun of their competition. What a great idea to improve their value equation.

## NISSAN ALTIMA: "Affordable Luxury"

At Chiat/Day, when we launched the Altima for Nissan in 1990, the conventional way to introduce it would have been to pit it against its direct competition, the Honda Accord and the Toyota Camry. But, Creative Director, Dick Sittig said, "Let's not compare this new model to its normal competition. Instead, let's position the Altima against the upscale Lexus Brand and call it Affordable Luxury."

In the television ad introducing the Altima, we used the exact same visual as the Lexus ad. We stacked champagne glasses on the hood of an Altima to demonstrate the smooth ride, quality, and luxury of the car, as the narrator read, "But when you buy the Altima, you'll still have plenty of money left over to buy the champagne. The new Altima from Nissan, starting at $22,000!"

## LEXUS, INFINITI: Creating a New Category

Nissan and Toyota wanted to attract customers who bought Mercedes and BMWs; however, they were aware that consumers were only going to pay so much money for the Nissan and Toyota brands. So, they had to create new brands to compete in the luxury segment.

Sometimes in marketing it's much easier to create a new brand than to get consumers to alter the current positioning images they have in their heads. To most automotive consumers, Nissan and Toyota were mid-level brands. The idea of creating Lexus for Toyota and Infiniti for Nissan was a great marketing idea. This allowed these companies to compete in the luxury segment of the automobile market where they could charge higher prices and get better margins, another great example of improving the value equation.

## WOLFGANG PUCK FOOD COMPANY

In 1985, Wolfgang Puck was a charming Austrian chef who owned a restaurant on Sunset Boulevard in

Hollywood named Spago, famous for its celebrity-filled after-parties the night of the Academy Awards.

Now in 2013, Wolfgang Puck is a major brand with restaurants, several lines of packaged goods, and a chain of fast-service pizza outlets called Wolfgang Puck Express. It all stemmed from the idea that since Wolfgang already had a successful name in the food business, why not expand the brand?

I was one of five people who created Wolfgang Puck Food Company with one product, frozen tarts. At the time, desserts were the only product that Wolfgang could make as a frozen-food item. He hadn't figured out yet how to manufacture frozen pizza.

Our initial retail sales came when we convinced the Neiman Marcus store in Beverly Hills to bring in a freezer case where we sold two frozen apple tarts in a package for five dollars. The major advertising used to generate awareness was a few sandwich boards that three employees and I wore as we walked along Rodeo Drive. We then created an event by having Wolfgang make a public appearance to sign autographs and sell tarts. Although this was not an easy sell, we were able to identify our target— upscale people who wanted to offer their dinner guests something unique.

Today, Wolfgang Puck Food Company has revenues of several hundreds of millions of dollars, and it all came from one single idea.

## SCORE: Libraries and Email Marketing

When I joined SCORE in 2002, the organization was doing a few seminars every year at National University in Costa Mesa. SCORE volunteer, Ed Reardon, decided to distribute brochures, promoting the seminars to libraries in the Orange County area.

At one branch, the librarian asked Ed if SCORE would put on a seminar in their library, adding that they had some federal grant money that would cover the cost. Ed accepted the librarian's offer, and in a matter of months he had signed up several more library branches that let us use their facilities. Suddenly our distribution system mushroomed from five locations to more than 240 seminars a year, reaching thousands of clients around Orange County alone.

By expanding our distribution system, combined with a new marketing tool called email, SCORE was able to increase the number of seminar attendees on an annual basis from a few hundred to several thousand.

## SCORE: Changing a Title Doubles Attendance

This is one of my favorite examples of how you can grow your business with just an idea and no money. I really mean "no money" for the idea or the execution.

For years, I gave a seminar for SCORE titled: How to Get and Keep More Customers. After two or three years with average response, I decided to see if I could increase the attendance at this seminar just by changing its name or title.

Nothing else about the seminar changed. The venue stayed the same. The promotion was still email marketing to the SCORE database. The price remained consistent at $30, as did the content of my presentation, and the presenter was still me. All I did was change the title from How to Get and Keep More Customers to Marketing without Money.

The result of this name change was that seminar attendance doubled. In other words, SCORE was able to increase its revenue by 100% just by changing a few words.

## GOT MILK?

Plain and simple, nobody thinks about milk until you're out. This insight led to a great marketing campaign.

## SUMMARY

As you can see in these ten examples, marketing is dependent upon ideas, not money. In each case, it was merely a matter of looking at a product, a service, or a brand with a fresh set of eyes. Even something as basic as renaming a seminar was used to help grow a business.

# WHAT MARKETING "IS" AND "IS NOT"

## Chapter 3

# WHAT MARKETING "IS NOT"

I'm going to mix things up a bit and start first with "What Marketing Is Not" simply because it's much easier to explain.

Most people think that marketing means advertising. While it's true that advertising is part of marketing, it is, in fact, minimal.

Think about how we perceive the world through our five senses: Hearing, Sight, Touch, Smell, and Taste. Suppose that for some horrible reason, you were denied the sense of sight, the ability to smell, and you couldn't hear. Imagine that the only one of your senses that you retained was the sense of taste. How limited would your world be? Sure, you could still enjoy a good meal, but you would be unable to see a beautiful sunset, hear a wonderful piece of music, or even smell the scent of a rosebud.

Now let's apply this same concept to marketing. If marketing were just advertising, it would be equally as limiting, like utilizing only one of your five senses.

# WHAT MARKETING "IS"

In the scope of the universe, marketing is so much more than advertising. Although promotional tools such as social media, television ads, direct-mail campaigns, and email can be useful in reaching consumers, marketing is more accurately defined as "everything you can do to attract and retain more good customers."

Marketing is about the products or services you provide and what consumer needs or wants they satisfy.

Marketing is about packaging; in other words, everything that people see about your product or service. It is about being attractive. If you offer a service, what do your offices look like? Is it located in an upscale law firm or a small space in a shopping mall? If you have a product, what kind of packaging does it come in? Is it in a special blue box similar to Tiffany's, or a brown paper bag like Chipotle Grill?

Marketing is about how you distribute your products or services; retail, wholesale, direct, or e-commerce. It's about convenience. How can you make it easier for your customers to purchase your product? Can consumers buy your product or service any time they want or need it, or do they have to wait for special office hours?

Marketing is about how you price your products or services and how you create value for the customer even though your price is higher than your competition.

Marketing is about how you promote your product or service. How do you position your product versus your competition? It's about generating awareness, consideration, purchase intent and closing the deal, and yes, it's about love. Creating a relationship in which your clients and customers love doing business with you persuades them to recommend your products and services to their friends.

Finally, marketing is all about targeting, which means getting your message to the right person, someone who is most likely to purchase your product or service based on their behaviors and values.

At the risk of being repetitive, I'll say it again. Marketing is more accurately defined as "everything you can do to attract and retain more good customers."

## GOOD MARKETING REQUIRES ABILITY

In the same way that everyone cannot play golf like Tiger Woods or the guitar like Eric Clapton, not every small-business owner has the ability to be outstanding at marketing.

I would argue, however, that in some way, all companies market their product or service. Some are simply much better at it than others, just as there are people who are more skillful at golf. That's not to say you can't be taught how to be a good marketer. It just takes developing the necessary skills and practice.

The first requirement of a good marketer is the ability to put someone else's needs in front of your own. This philosophy has been around for thousands of years and probably more familiar to you as "The Golden Rule: Do unto others as you would have them do unto you."

Another important skill, and what all successful marketing is based on, is being able to figure out what people want or need. Phil Knight at Nike teamed up with Bill Bowerman when he created the Waffle Trainer shoe to satisfy the desire for better shoe cushions for long-distance runners. Steve Jobs and Steve Wozniak created the first Apple computer to make it less complicated for the average person to access the power of computing.

Good marketers also understand the difference between rational and emotional needs. Knowing that consumers will buy products and services that help them look, feel, and do better in some activity, it is the job of a good marketer to inform consumers how their products or services fulfill these desires.

| Rational Need | Emotional Need |
|---|---|
| I need a new pair of shoes because my old shoes are worn out. | I need a new pair of shoes because they make me feel better. |

Additionally, good marketers understand that their products and/or services will not appeal to everyone. Many multi-billion-dollar companies started out with just a tiny share of the total market. For many years, Apple had only about 5% of the computer market. Nissan has only about 6% or 7% of the market for new automobile sales. Good marketers do not waste money trying to convince everyone to buy their products. Nike is not for everyone, nor is Apple or Nissan. You cannot be everything to everyone. But, you can be something to someone.

Volvo drivers prefer safety over styling. BMW customers want the ultimate driving machine. Apple positioned their Macintosh computer as "the computer for the rest of us." They also spend a lot of money differentiating their "cool" customers from those who buy PCs.

Possessing an innate knowledge, good marketers know what their customers need and want. Steve Jobs didn't use focus groups because he knew what his customers wanted in a computer. Fortunately for him, it was the same thing he wanted—more power, more appeal, speed, easier to use, and wonderful to hold in your hand—all much more cool.

Phil Knight, CEO and Founder of Nike, said when we were introducing the Air Jordan basketball shoe, "If someone doesn't know who Michael Jordan is, they are not our customer."

Phil Knight didn't need focus groups either because basically, the entire staff at Nike were athletes, so it makes sense that they all knew what they wanted—better performance, a competitive advantage, and gear. In essence, they wanted to win. It wasn't about being cool. It was about sweat, hard work, dedication, and getting up at 5:00 a.m. to go running like 1984 Olympic Gold Medal Marathon Winner, Joan Benoit.

Unfortunately, not every small-business owner is going to have the same marketing ability as Steve Jobs or Phil Knight. However, that doesn't mean you can't improve your marketing skills.

The good news about marketing is that, at the very basic level, it's simple. It's not brain surgery. It's not rocket science. It's innate within everyone. In fact, you already know how to do it.

You don't need to get a college degree to learn how to market. You don't need to attend seminars or read books about the subject (except maybe this one) because you already know how to do it. You've been doing it for most of your life. You just need to learn how to tap into it.

## ATTRACTION DEFINED

The essence of marketing is about creating attraction. The verb "attract" is defined as 1) the ability to draw or direct to oneself by some quality or action, 2) to evoke interest or admiration in, and 3) to be magnetic or alluring.

## MARKETING IS ALL ABOUT BEING ATTRACTIVE

At some point in our lives we have all tried to make ourselves attractive to someone else. Generally, this desire begins about the time we reach puberty. If we could remember what we did 10, 20, 30 years ago to try to make ourselves more attractive to someone else, we would automatically know how to be better at marketing.

In my seminars, I play a game called "The Attraction Game", using myself as the "product" to make it fun and down to earth. The object of "The Attraction Game" is to try to make me, the product or service, more attractive. I am a 68-year-old, short, white male with a beard and a baseball cap, and at times I look like a homeless person. This really is just a game, as I am very happily married.

I start by asking what could be done to improve my appeal. In many of my seminars, some very smart person usually asks, "To whom do you want to be more attractive?" I am always delighted to hear this because it's the absolutely correct question to be asking first. Before we can figure out how to make ourselves or our product/ service more attractive, we have to ask, "Attractive to whom?"

This, of course, refers to the Target Audience, about which I will cover later in this book. For now, let's move on.

For a person, product or service, there are basically five areas in which we can increase our appeal or desirability:

- Packaging (Everything people see)
- Product or Service (Our character/personality)
- Distribution (How accessible are we?)
- Value (Benefits vs. cost or baggage)
- Promotion (Be better known)

## PACKAGING

The first and easiest way to be more attractive is to improve our physical appearance. In other words, focus on how we look. We do this all the time. If you want to sell your car, you probably get it washed and detailed. If you're selling your house, you may have it painted and replace the carpet. You do things to make it look better.

In marketing lingo, this is called packaging. In my seminars, I tell people that packaging is everything that people see about your business.

Getting back to "The Attraction Game", let me list some of the answers given in my seminar when I ask what I could do to improve my physical appearance. How can I improve my packaging?

- Shave the beard; get a haircut
- Better clothes
- Lose the baseball cap
- Smile more often
- Get my teeth fixed
- Get in better physical shape

Notice that some of these things, like smile more often, are free—marketing without money—and a few come at a price, such as fixing my teeth. The important thing to remember about packaging, however, is that making things look good is just one piece of the puzzle.

## PRODUCT OR SERVICE

Another way we can make ourselves more attractive is to improve the product. Obviously, this is generally more complicated than merely improving the packaging. In the case of a person, it means having a better personality or character. I'd have to be more likeable; maybe more trustworthy, dependable, attentive, and concerned about the needs of others.

The following are some of the suggestions I have received from people attending my seminars about how I could improve my performance as a human being. (Keep in mind that my wife can give me a much longer and more comprehensive list):

- Be funny and charming
- Be honest and trustworthy
- Don't be self-centered
- Don't be so intense
- Be more gregarious

In business, as is the case with most people, improving the performance of a product or service usually generates greater success than merely improving the packaging. I may get a better wardrobe and a haircut, but no one is going to be very attracted to me if I'm a jerk.

## DISTRIBUTION

A third way of becoming more attractive has to do with making it more convenient for people to encounter me. If I stay home every night, it's unlikely that I am going to find someone who will be attracted to me. I would have to get out more and go to the right places. In marketing, this translates to having a better distribution system, making it easier for people to access your goods or services.

Here are some of the suggestions I get when I ask, "How can I improve my distribution system?"

- Join an online dating service
- Go to a bar, a gym, a dance
- Attend community events
- Go where you'll meet those with common interests

As you will see in this book, some of the most dramatic and impressive business gains in sales and revenue came from companies improving and expanding their distribution systems, which made it more convenient for people to do business with them.

## VALUE

The fourth way to be more attractive is to improve your value equation: "Value = Benefits Divided by Cost." In this math equation, the numerator is the benefit and the denominator is the cost or price. In a good value equation, you get a lot of benefits for a very low cost.

SCORE is a perfect example of a very good value equation. The client gets free counseling, his or her only cost being their time and travel expense. On the other hand, a middle-aged man who is paying alimony to four ex-wives and has five children to put through college is a very bad value equation at the personal level.

Fortunately, I am neither divorced nor paying alimony, but the following are some of the ideas I have received about how I can improve my value equation:

- Own a nice car
- Have a lot of money
- Be willing to sign a pre-nuptial agreement guaranteeing a million dollars

## PROMOTION

The fifth and final thing we have to do to be more attractive is to be better known. This is called promotion, and what most people consider to be marketing. As you can see, however, it's just one of the several ways we can make ourselves or our business more attractive.

When I talk about promotion, I always start with the Purchase Process or the Purchase Funnel, which we will discuss in much greater detail in Chapter 11. But, for the sake of "The Attraction Game", here are some questions I would need to ask that pertain to the Purchase Funnel for me, the product:

- How many people in my target audience are aware that Tom exists? (AWARENESS)

- How many people would consider going out with Tom? (CONSIDERATION)

- How many people would still consider going out with Tom after they have shopped around? (SHOPPING)

- How many people intend to go out with Tom? (INTENTION)

- How many people have gone out with Tom? (BUY)

- How many people who have gone out with Tom would go out again? (LOVE)

The first thing you need to concentrate on is AWARENESS. In small businesses, most owners start out in what I call "The Pit Of Non-Awareness." Quite literally, no one knows that they exist.

In "The Attraction Game", the following are some of the suggestions I get about how I can promote myself:

- Join LinkedIn
- Create a Facebook Page
- Start a Blog
- Get some publicity written about me

The point of "The Attraction Game" is to get you to realize that you already know about marketing. In fact, you've been doing it most of your life. It's not scary. It's not complicated. But, to do it well, it does require some skill and intuition, as well as practice and patience.

In Chapter 6: Marketing Leverage, we will take a look at some of the examples of how successful companies utilized these five basic ways to make their products or services more attractive.

# WHAT YOU NEED
# TO KNOW
# ABOUT SOCIAL MEDIA

.

## Chapter 4

# WHAT YOU NEED TO KNOW ABOUT SOCIAL MEDIA

You can't talk about promoting your product or service nowadays without bringing up social media. It has grown so quickly into such a vital marketing tool. Everywhere you look—television commercials, magazine articles, the nightly news, cell phones—social media has impacted almost every aspect of our lives.

Admittedly, at times I've downplayed the importance of social media, probably because I'm not as technologically savvy as most. But rest assured, everything I teach you in *Marketing Without Money* can work in conjunction with this revolutionary communication tool.

While I don't claim to be an expert at social media, I have read many books and attended several seminars and workshops and I get the basic concept of what it's all about. But, other than my Facebook page, *Tom Patty's Marketing Without Money*, YouTube videos, and my email account with Constant Contact, I have very little personal knowledge of, or experience with, social media. I don't have a MySpace account; I don't check for discounts on my iPhone, and I'm not a member of LinkedIn. In other words, I'm certainly not in a position to give advice about how you can use social media to grow your business.

Having said that, I do have opinions about the role of social media in marketing.

Social media is truly a revolutionary event in the history of civilization, inverting the old paradigm of authority figures; "We Talk—You Listen", by providing the masses with a voice.

Its arrival is as significant as the Copernicus Revolution; in effect, declaring that those same authority figures are not the center of the universe, just as Copernicus proclaimed the Earth was not located in the center of our solar system.

In both the real world and cyberspace, effective communication is imminent where marketing is concerned. Communication is not just what you say, but how and where you say it, what people hear, and how they respond. In other words, it's a two-way process.

For most of my lifetime, communicating through advertising was a one-way street. Advertisers spent tons of money telling you why you should buy Tide Detergent or Hoover Vacuum Cleaners. This was not a dialogue. It was a monologue.

Nowadays, advertising is much more of a conversation with the consumer, who is now smarter, more sophisticated, and savvy. Because of all of the technological advances in the past 10 years, consumers know what your competitors offer and how your products or services compare. It is no longer effective to try to beat the message into their heads.

When I first entered the advertising business in 1978, there were a handful of communication methods: television, radio, billboards, and print. Now there are hundreds of ways to reach consumers. Thanks to the Internet, we can add Google, Facebook, Twitter, YouTube, etc. to the list.

However, in today's business world there are so many communication tools that it gets overwhelming at times, leaving novice marketers confused about where to go and what to do first.

## WHAT IS SOCIAL MEDIA?

Before we get too far into this discussion, according to Wikipedia, social media is defined as "social software which mediates human communication." [5] By this definition, a telephone is part of social media.

Tim Grahl, founder of www.OutThinkGroup.com, defines the following types of social media:

- Social Networks (Facebook, LinkedIn)
- Bookmarking Sites (Delicious, Stumbled Upon)
- Social News (Digg, Reddit)
- Media Sharing (YouTube, Twitter)
- Micro Blogging (Twitter)
- Blog Comments and Forums (WordPress, etc.) [6]

Thankfully, there are ranking systems that attempt to sort out and define the most popular social-media sites, with the majority listing Facebook, YouTube, MySpace, Twitter, Flicker, and LinkedIn in the Top Ten. In reality, however, there are literally hundreds of networks and channels.

## HOW IS SOCIAL MEDIA DIFFERENT FROM TRADITIONAL MEDIA?

The primary distinction between social and traditional media is the cost. We all know how expensive a

5   12 January 2013 <http://en.wikipedia.org/wiki/Social_media_patent>
Social Media
6   12 January 2013 <http://outthinkgroup.com>, Tim Grahl

30-second television commercial is on the Super Bowl or the Academy Awards. On the other hand, one of the biggest reasons everyone (especially a small-business owner) is attracted to the concept of social media is that it can help to increase awareness of their product or service without literally spending a dime.

This belief is backed up by actual research conducted by the Harvard Business Review Analytic Services, which published a study about the perceived benefits of social media by business owners. According to "The New Conversation: Taking Social Media from Talk to Action", published in the *Harvard Business Review*, August 2010, 59% of those surveyed claimed that the primary benefit was increased awareness, followed by 39% who claimed increased traffic to website. This is the main reason why most people are attracted to my seminar, Marketing Without Money. They believe that social media is the answer to creating more awareness.

While social media may be an excellent way to achieve awareness, it has not yet been proven to generate more good customers or grow your business. In fact, the same Harvard Business School study, cited above, found that only 11% of those surveyed said they saw any increase in new business. Another 11% claimed that they did not derive any benefit from social media.

For now, however, rather than focus on the differences between social and traditional media, I will recognize their similarities.

## A MEDIUM IS A VEHICLE TO CARRY A MESSAGE

The first thing to understand about any type of media is that it is a vehicle. A media vehicle carries a message, just as a car carries a driver and passengers. As with a car, the driver is much more important than the vehicle because the driver determines and directs where and how the vehicle travels to its destination. In other words, the driver is the master and the media vehicle is the servant— doing what the driver wants.

In my seminars I like to say, "If you don't know how to drive a car, getting a new Ferrari won't make you a better driver." The important point here is that social media, just as with all other media, is only effective in the hands of someone who knows how to use its strengths and can live within its limitations.

All media have certain advantages and limitations. An outdoor billboard cannot effectively communicate a long complicated message, but a letter can. A Twitter message can contain only 140 characters, but it has the potential to reach millions of people in a matter of seconds.

Many times, my SCORE clients ask if they should use Facebook, Twitter, direct mail, or run ads in the local newspaper. I always tell them that it depends on the answers to the following questions:

• With whom are you trying to communicate?
• What is the nature of your message? Is it simple or complex?

Let's deal with the second issue first. What is the nature of your message? Is it simple or complex?

A simple message like "Got Milk?" can be effectively communicated in almost any medium. We all know the famous advertising campaign created by the ad agency, Weiden and Kennedy. The "Got Milk?" slogan was communicated effectively on outdoor billboards, television and print ads, and practically all other media. It was brilliant.

But a more complicated message, like why you should buy a new car, may require more words than you can fit on a Twitter feed or a billboard.

Next, you must ask, "With whom am I trying to communicate?

In today's world, we are seeing that fewer and fewer young people are watching television. The demographics of TV viewers are skewing older each year. If you want to reach a more mature audience, television is a great way to connect with your target. On the other hand, it may not be ideal for capturing the attention of the youth.

This is not just about demographics, however. There is another issue going on here—behavior. In this new world we live in, there is a divide that separates people. Actually, it is more of a continuum from people who are highly connected to those who are less in touch.

We all have friends who cannot be separated from their cell phones or who have to check their email every three minutes. There are also those who use a cell phone only for calling their spouse and can easily live without email for days or weeks.

Of course, there are exceptions, but generally, elderly people are less connected than the youth of today.

As a small-business owner you need to ask yourself the following questions: "Who is my target audience? Do I want to spend a lot of time and energy trying to reach people who are highly connected?" If these people are important to you, then it is critical that you become proficient at social media. On the other hand, if your target audience is older and less connected, it may not be a priority for you to get too involved in honing your social-media skills.

To summarize, social media is a vehicle of communication. Before you can effectively use it, however, you need to become proficient with the basic concepts of marketing, just as you need to master driving a car before you get behind the wheel of a Ferrari.

## THEY CALL IT SOCIAL MEDIA BECAUSE IT'S SOCIAL

The second point I want to make about social media is that it's social.  It is not really designed to "sell stuff."

To demonstrate this important reality, imagine for a moment that you are hosting a dinner party at your house. You invite several guests, carefully selecting those whom you think will enjoy each other's company and conversation. Your job as host or hostess is to make sure that everyone of your guests has an enjoyable evening. You can only imagine how awkward and out of place it would be if one of your friends used this social occasion to try to sell life-insurance policies to the other guests. The environment is wrong. In many ways, social media is more like a dinner party than a marketplace.

Unfortunately, many small-business owners don't realize until after they create a Facebook page for their business, how limited it is as a selling tool. It's much more vital as a cyber-bulletin board, a way to direct potential customers to your website. Facebook friends aren't there to buy; they're there to socialize.

## THE RULES ARE DIFFERENT

One reason that some of my clients don't understand how to use social media as a marketing tool is that they are still thinking in the old paradigm. They use social media in the same way that they could use television, radio, print or outdoor ads to communicate, convince, and persuade.

The one thing I am certain of is that social media is much more participatory than the traditional media. It is about relationships and friendships and sharing, not selling propositions.

## DON'T GET BOGGED DOWN IN SOCIAL MEDIA

The third and most important point I want to make clear about social media is that getting involved can be a huge diversion and possibly an inefficient use of time for the small-business owner or entrepreneur.

Trying to become an expert in social media can absorb an enormous amount of time and energy—going to seminars, reading books, and attempting to learn everything there is to know about all of the social networks. I have seen so many of my SCORE clients spending hundreds of hours learning about social media. They believe that if they could just figure out how to use the holy grail of promotion, their business would explode. Generally, these people end up with little or no positive benefit to their business.

## WHAT SHOULD I DO?

My recommendation is to focus. You need to concentrate on running your business, not fooling around too much with social media. If you do venture into the world of cyberspace, you should pick one vehicle and get really good at it. Facebook, Twitter, LinkedIn—you need to decide which one your business will benefit from most.

When my clients ask me for my personal recommendation, I tell them to focus on email marketing and YouTube. That's not to say the other forms of social media don't produce results. I am just more familiar with these two. It's been my experience that they provide me with the biggest bang for my buck.

Email marketing is virtually the only tool that SCORE utilizes. When I joined SCORE 10 years ago, we had no database, email activity was non-existent. Today, our chapter sends out hundreds of thousands of emails every year. According to Constant Contact (an email database management system that allows members to send mail spam-free), our SCORE chapter is one of their most active customers.

If you are included in SCORE 114's database you know how many email messages you receive a month, announcing the date, the location and title for the more than 200 various seminars and workshops happening around the Orange County area every year. This email marketing program has allowed us to grow our business exponentially, from literally zero to tens of thousands of people in the past seven years.

## THE POWER OF SOCIAL MEDIA

One of my favorite stories about the power of social media concerns a singer/ songwriter named Dave Carroll, who was traveling to a gig with his band, Sons of Maxwell, and his beloved $3,500 Taylor guitar. Even before boarding the United Air-  lines flight from Halifax, Nova Scotia, to Chicago, the neck on his guitar was broken by the baggage handlers.

Dave complained to the United Airlines Customer Service Department and insisted that they provide some kind of recompense, preferably a new guitar.

Basically being told by United to "pound sand and go away," Dave responded, "If you don't satisfy my claim, I am going to write a song about you and post it on YouTube."

Unfortunately for the airline, the threat was not taken seriously and in the summer of 2009 the executives at United were surprised to see that after only one day, 150,000 people had watched Carroll's two-minute video on YouTube, "United Breaks Guitars." As of the publication of this book, the video has had over 12,827,200 hits.

This story has a wonderfully happy ending—for Dave, that is. Eventually, United gave him enough money to buy a new guitar. Dave's cute little song and video also catapulted him from the pit of non-awareness to that of a minor celebrity. He was additionally inundated with new opportunities for singing gigs. But the most interesting part of Dave's story is that he became sought after as a consultant and speaker on the subject of "How to Improve Customer Service." He has also recently written a great book on his experience, appropriately called, "United Breaks Guitars." [7]

---

7  Dave Carroll, "United Breaks Guitars: The Power of One Voice in the Age of Social Media" (Hay House 2012)

# BACK TO BASICS:

*Is There a Market for Your Goods or Services?*

# Chapter 5

# BACK TO BASICS:

## *Is There a Market for Your Goods or Services?*

Every year, I sit down face-to-face with hundreds of small-business owners and entrepreneurs who come to me for help and advice with their marketing. Some of these people are not yet in business, but they have an idea or maybe they own a patent for a new invention that they want to sell. My initial questions to these people are:

- Who is going to buy this new product or service?
- What evidence is there that a market exists?

But let's not get ahead of ourselves. First off, what is a market? No, I am not talking about a local supermarket or the stock market. I am talking about the overall market for goods and/or services.

## FIRST COMPONENT OF A MARKET:
## New Product/Service

As a SCORE counselor, I hear about several new ideas every year—some good and solid, others not so good. Recently, I met with a couple who want to sell glass straws to save the environment. Is there a market for glass straws? I don't know. That's their job to find out.

My favorite example of a new product that created a new market was the introduction of the stand-up paddleboard. Since the late 1800s, surfboards have been carved and shaped to stand up on and surf down the face of a wave. Paddleboards were bigger, heavier, and built to lie prone and paddle with your arms and shoulders. Except for a few surfers in Hawaii (most notably, Duke Kahanamoku), almost no one stood up to paddle.

When I first saw people down in the Dana Point Marina paddling their stand-up paddleboards, I thought it was the dumbest thing I had ever seen. Why would anyone want to do this? If someone had come to me as a SCORE client and asked my opinion about the market for stand-up paddleboards, I would have told them it was insignificant.

Of course, it turns out that I was totally wrong (once again, as my wife would say). Stand-up paddleboards just happen to be a hugely successful market that is growing exponentially, and just to prove how wrong I was, I actually went out and bought one for myself.

After literally getting my feet wet, I now see that it makes perfect sense. Surfing requires waves, which usually means you have to be near an ocean, a definite geographic limitation. It also requires ability, balance, strength, and tenacity. Surfing was one of the most difficult sports I ever tried to master back when I was a kid growing up in Newport Beach. Stand-up paddling, on the other hand, is something almost anyone can do relatively easily and quickly. In addition, and more importantly, it can be done anywhere there is water—rivers, lakes, etc.

## SECOND COMPONENT OF A MARKET: Customers

To the small-business owner, a "market" means that there is a demand for some specific goods or services. According to my dictionary, "demand" is defined as "the desire to possess something, confirmed by the ability to purchase it." I love this definition so much, I want you to repeat it out loud: "Demand is the desire to possess something, confirmed by the ability to purchase it."

Basically, demand is more than just wishing you had something. It is about wanting something and being able to pay for it.

The second component of a market is a group of people who are willing to pay for a product or service. I call these people "customers."

When I was a young man in the 1960s there were many people who surfed, rode bicycles, and did tricks on skateboards, but they didn't get paid to do it. There was no market for professional surfers, mountain bikers or skateboarders. Today, of course, this has changed and there are a number of people who make millions of dollars performing these activities.

Markets can also be separated into different categories. There are separate markets for automobiles, watches, milk, and everything else you can think of that is sold today.

In addition, a market can be segmented into even smaller units or sub-markets. For example, in the automobile market there are SUVs, sports cars, hybrids, and low-priced vehicles.

Finally, and most important, markets are constantly changing. Some markets and market segments are thriving while others are declining. There are mature markets and those that are emerging. I know that it may be difficult to imagine, but at one time, the sale of automobiles was an emerging market. If you think about it, for the majority of the 20th Century, there weren't markets for personal computers, tablets, or even smartphones.

Sometimes people create a product or service even though there is no evidence of a sustainable market. A few of these people go on to create huge market demand and, as a result, they are handsomely rewarded, financially. We can all think of obvious examples: Henry Ford, Bill Gates, Steve Jobs, etc.

Others have created new products or categories such as bell-bottomed jeans and Pet Rocks that sold extremely well for a period of time then sales dropped off precipitously. In marketing terms, these are known as fads.

Your first job as a marketer is to make an assessment of the market potential for your product or service. Is this demand a long-term trend (running shoes), or is it just a fad (Pet Rock)? In what segment of the market will your product or service be operating, and is this segment growing or declining?

You might remember that in the first part of this book I talked about my failure as an entrepreneur. You may also recall that one of the reasons why I failed so miserably was because I had not really done enough good, hard research of the market for music CDs.

In hindsight, the CD market in 2000 was not growing and in fact, had begun to shows signs of decline. While new forms of listening devices like Napster, LimeWire, and other Internet companies provided free downloads, MP3 players filled the shelves in local retail stores. Even the giants in the record industry were having a hard time selling CDs. Small independent artists like me did not have a chance.

As a specific example, let's look at Zappos and their new, bold and interesting concept of selling shoes on the Internet. As you can imagine, when they first talked with investors they did not get a warm reception. The conventional wisdom was that nobody would buy shoes on the Internet. You had to be able to try on the shoes and see how they felt before you would commit to purchasing.

In fact, when Tony Hsieh, the CEO of Zappos, was first approached as a possible investor, he writes in his book, *Delivering Happiness*, "it sounded like the poster child of bad Internet ideas," like selling pet food online. [8]

To make a long story short, Tony invested in the company, whereupon they instituted a policy that allowed customers to order several pairs of shoes at a time and return the ones they didn't like or that didn't fit, without any shipping charge. Ten years later, Zappos was sold to Amazon for $1.2 billion.

One of the reasons Tony was so successful was because he asked the right question: "In what segment of the market will this company have to compete?" After doing some research, Tony discovered that the overall footwear industry in the U.S. alone was a $40 billion business. But the really interesting fact was that a market segment already existed where people were buying shoes from paper mail-order catalogs. This was in itself a $2 billion business, about 5% of the total market.

Tony figured he could do a better job of selling shoes than the catalogs, and it turned out that he was right. In fact, he proved that he could compete favorably selling shoes, not just in the mail-order segment, but to people who had never before bought shoes by mail.

---

8  Tony Hsieh and Rob Ten Pas, "Delivering Happiness: A Path to Profits, Passion, and Purpose" (A Round Table Comic, Writers of the Round Table Press 2012)

## THIRD COMPONENT OF A MARKET: Competition

Another thing you need to be thinking about is, against whom are you going to be competing? Not only do you have to be aware of competition within a given market, but what kind of threats could come from the outside.

Blockbuster's main competitive threat did not come from within the video rental business, but rather outside the market in the form of NetFlix. The same is true with Border's Books. Their main threat was the online presence of Amazon, not competing retail bookstores.

It is always discouraging to me when I ask small-business owners who their competition is and they answer, "We don't really have any." In reality, almost everyone has either direct or indirect competition.

If you operate a cruise line, you not only have direct competition from the other cruise lines—Norwegian, Carnival, etc.—but you are also competing with alternate forms of vacation travel.

### SUMMARY:  Back to Basics

To determine whether there is a market for your idea, business or service, periodically ask yourself the following questions:

1. What is my product or service? What does it do for people? How does it make their life better? (Your answer needs to be comprehensible to a five-year-old.)

2. Who will buy my product or service? What do they desire? What do they lack? What do they value?

3. Is there an existing market? If so, how big is the total annual dollar revenue?

4. What are the important market segments? Which segments are growing and which are declining?

5. Is this market sustainable or is it a fad?

6. Against whom in this market will I have to compete?

7. Why will customers buy my product or service versus the competition?

# PART II:
# HOW?

# MARKETING LEVERAGE

**"THE BIG 5"**
**STRATEGIES**
(Big Levers)

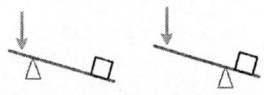

1. Solve more needs/wants
2. Be more attractive
3. Be more convenient
4. Be a better value
5. Be better known (funnel)

## Chapter 6

# MARKETING LEVERAGE

### *How Other Companies Used*
### *"The Big 5" to Grow Their Businesses*

In 400 BCE the Greek mathematician and philosopher Archimedes said, "Give me a lever long enough and a fulcrum to place it on and I will move the world."

Archimedes was talking about the concept of leverage. He was the first to explain how a large weight could more easily be lifted with the use of a rigid lever and a properly placed fulcrum. (Refer to the graphic on the preceding page.)

According to the OED, "leverage" is defined as 1) "advantage for accomplishing a purpose, and 2) increased power of action."

There are many kinds of leverage. There's financial leverage, engineering leverage, and political leverage. But what we want to focus on here is marketing leverage, which is the ability to achieve a large increase in revenues and sales from a relatively small outlay of money.

As a small-business owner, the concept of marketing leverage should be very important to you. You do not have a large staff or a big marketing budget, so you must try to use every possible advantage you can find to make your efforts and your money more effective and efficient.

## "THE BIG 5"

In the history of the world (at least going back to the days of Archimedes) there have been five marketing strategies that have been proven to be the most successful ways to achieve marketing leverage.

This list of five strategies is responsible for the success of Apple, Nike, Starbucks, Amazon, and hundreds of other prosperous companies:

- Solve more consumer needs or wants
- Be more attractive
- Be more convenient
- Be a better value
- Be better known

The first thing you probably noticed is that these strategies are very similar, in fact identical to the discussion we had about ways you could make yourself more attractive in "The Attraction Game."

For you more mature small-business owners, you may also notice that these same strategies mirror the old marketing concept of "The 5 Ps," that was taught in every business school in the 1950s and 1960s. In the middle of the 20th Century at the Harvard Business School, "The 5 Ps" were defined as Product, Packaging, Place (Distribution), Price, and Promotion, and considered to be the basic elements of business marketing—just as the basic elements of an internal combustion engine include a fuel pump, a carburetor, and spark plugs.

The idea back at Harvard was that in order to start or run a business, you needed to have all of these "Ps" figured out. In the 1950s, the most sophisticated and intelligent marketing was done by the giants in the "packaged goods" category. Companies like Proctor & Gamble, Kraft Foods, and General Mills were considered the icons of marketing knowledge and expertise. The goal of many students at the Harvard Business School was one day to be a Brand Manager at a company like P&G.

Many things have changed since then. First, the level of competition has increased dramatically. When I graduated from college, I had to compete against other kids from the United States. Now, a college graduate has to go up against exceptionally bright, talented, and motivated students from all over the world. As Thomas Friedman explains, "There are now two billion more people in China and India against whom we now have to compete." [9]

Let's look more closely at these five strategies and some specific examples of how each has been implemented in the real world. Below is a great chart that has converted "The 5 Ps" into "The Big 5" for continuity's sake and to give you a visual.

| "The 5Ps" | "The Big 5" | Your Business/ Service | Customer/ Client |
|---|---|---|---|
| New Products | Solve More Consumer Needs/ Wants | What problem does it solve? | How is it better than your competition? |
| Packaging | Be More Attractive | How can you make it more attractive? | How is it better than your competition? |
| Place (Distribution) | Be More Convenient | How can you make it easier to purchase? | How is it better than your competition? |
| Price | Create a Better Value | What is the value equation? | How is it better than your competition? |
| Promotion | Be Better Known | How can I move consumers down the Purchase Funnel? | How is it better than your competition? |

9 Thomas Friedman, "The World is Flat 3.0: A Brief History of the Twenty-First Century" (Picador 2007)

At the end of the chapter, you can fill in a chart like this for your own business, showing how each of "The Big 5" answers a specific need for your customer or consumer. But for now, let's take a look at each of "The Big 5" strategies one by one.

## STRATEGY #1: Solve More Consumer Needs/Wants by Introducing New Products or Services

Obviously, one of the best examples of this strategy is Apple. They consistently come out with products that solve consumer needs. Apple is so brilliant at it that they are able to identify and solve needs even before the customer realizes they want it.

I remember what my life was like before there was such a product as an iPod. Whenever I traveled, I carried with me a Sony Discman. Sure, I also had to bring along all the discs that I wanted to listen to, but I was pretty content because I didn't know there was a better option. Then Apple introduced the iPod and iTunes. Now I could download my entire music collection onto one tiny little machine that fits in my pocket.

Let's also think about the iPod, the iPhone, and the iPad and their appeal. Then consider how they solve the needs and wants of consumers. Apple has even gone so far as to create new needs by making their own products obsolete. Everyone was happy with the iPhone 4 until the iPhone 5 was introduced.

Nike is another great example of a company that has grown its business by solving more customer needs. Initially, Nike sold track shoes to athletes who ran on track teams. With the introduction of the Waffle Trainer shoe, Nike offered a new exciting product for recreational runners and was able to greatly expand their business. Then Nike introduced the Air Jordan for people who played basketball. Today, Nike offers solutions for all kinds of athletic endeavors, from running to football to golf, you name it.

When I was working with the Wolfgang Puck Food Company, our first product was frozen desserts. By adding frozen pizzas to our product line we were able to greatly grow the business and satisfy many more consumer needs and wants.

This strategy of satisfying more consumer needs works equally well for service-oriented companies. When I was at Chiat/Day, we created new opportunities for clients to pay us more money. In addition to traditional media advertising, the agency created a Direct Marketing Division, a separate Media Buying Group, and a division that specialized in Internet Marketing.

At SCORE, in addition to solving more of our clients' needs by offering seminars, workshops and one-on-one counseling, we created our CEO Forums where volunteer executives can benefit from peer-to-peer discussions. We were able to satisfy women business owners, as well, by creating the Women's Breakfast and the Annual Women in Business Conference where they can network and learn.

The key to utilizing this strategy effectively is to make sure that the new products or services are aligned with the core essence of your brand. Every product Apple introduces, reinforces the essence of Apple: ease of use, aesthetic design, innovative technology, with the added bonus of the cool factor in a new manifestation.

The same is true with Nike. Each new product delivers the essence of the Nike brand promise: enhanced athletic performance, whether it's a running shoe or the newest running tech gadget. This is not the same as just creating new products or new divisions like a conglomerate. Everything has to be another manifestation of the brand promise.

But what if you are just starting out and you have only one product? How can you apply this strategy? It's simple. You need to understand what consumer needs and wants your product or service actually satisfies.

Let's say you want to start a company that imports ladies' handbags made in Indonesia, like one of my SCORE clients, Laga Bags. There are thousands of attractive, well-made bags on the market. So, we had to figure out what made these bags special.

After attending several trade shows, the two founders of Laga Bags, Roy and Louise van Broekhuizen, discovered that quilters were especially impressed with the handmade aspect. This critical discovery guided their whole marketing effort and has helped them grow their company from zero to over $1 million in annual revenues. They discovered that their products could satisfy the needs and wants of a whole new group of people—Quilters.

In the beginning, it's important to learn what people are buying. When we started Wolfgang Puck Food Company we were surprised to learn that our upscale clients in Beverly Hills weren't paying for frozen pastries; they were buying a piece of Wolfgang Puck, the famous chef of Spago, and a little touch of celebrity. This understanding was the basis for the marketing of all of their new products: frozen pizza, canned soups, and Wolfgang Puck Express Restaurants in airport terminals.

## STRATEGY #2:  Be More Attractive (Packaging)

It is easy to understand what packaging means when it comes to cans of vegetables and cereal boxes, or for that matter anything that comes in a package. But the reality is that everything sold, every product and service, has a packaging component.

On a cross-country airline flight from New York to Los Angeles, Jay Chiat found himself sitting next to architect, Frank Gehry. By the time the plane landed, Jay had asked Frank to design a new office building in Venice, California. Frank Gehry commissioned the famous sculptor, Klaus Oldenberg, to create a giant pair of binoculars for the entry into the driveway. It was so unique that our building became known as "The Binocular Building", which spurred prospective clients to call us up and ask if they could get a tour. This turned out to be a pretty good opportunity for a business pitch. Our office building became part of our packaging.

One of my current clients is a window cleaner named Chris. His packaging is his pickup truck that displays colorful graphics and his tagline, "It's Window Cleaning Time." Also, instead of business cards, Chris gives each of his clients a ballpoint pen with his logo, his slogan, and his phone number. What a great calling card! I never need to look up Chris' number to schedule an appointment. It's right on my desk.

Another of my SCORE clients has created a whole new concept for the packaging of wine. His company, "Stacked Wine", includes four individual glasses stacked on top of one another. This is a terrific example of creating a more attractive and useful package.

One of my favorite stories about packaging has to do with a present I bought my wife. We had gone to Monte Carlo and visited the Grace Kelly Museum where I was first introduced to the "Kelly Bag" made by Hermes. These bags are very expensive and hard to find. But eventually, while we were on a river cruise in Europe, I located a store that had a large inventory in the town of Nuremberg, Germany. My wife picked out the bag she wanted and that evening at dinner we took the box to the ship's restaurant to share our prize with our shipboard friends. Before we even opened the box, people started gathering around the table commenting, "Oh my goodness, it's a Hermes box. You must have done something really bad." By the end of dinner, several people had asked if they could have the box. Can you believe it? Even the packaging was in high demand!

Of course, the most famous and wonderful story about new packaging is what happened in the bottled-water industry. When I was a kid in the 1950s and 1960s, bottled water came in five-gallon glass bottles that were delivered by a truck to your house, the two most visible brands being Arrowhead and Sparklett's. The delivery man would hoist the heavy and awkward container onto his shoulder, lug it into the house, and set it on the cooler. This was how bottled water was packaged. Now, fast forward to today. Almost everyone carries an eight-ounce bottle of water with them everywhere they go—in the car, their purse, the baby carriage, on a run, in the gym. Water has become portable and mobile.

It's unbelievable just how much the world has changed since I was a kid. Back then I used to pay for music, buying albums and 45s of my favorite groups, and I drank water for free out of the tap. Now, I pay for water, 36 bottles at a time, and music is free (well, almost, on iTunes.)

Here are some additional examples of how businesses have grown by creating new, more attractive or functional packaging:

• Some companies that make toothpaste and ketchup have created new packaging that allows the container to stand in an upside-down position that facilitates the flow of the product, an age-old problem as any ketchup lover can tell you.

• Airlines have painted their planes with interesting graphics. The airplane, along with the boarding pass, the flight attendants, the fabric and the texture of the seats are all part of the packaging of their service.

• SCORE 114 has created a whole new design concept for the thousands of emails they send out. Every email you receive from SCORE is part of the packaging.

• Apple is such a great example because they do everything right. In terms of packaging, Apple products are all about how things look and feel. From the clean modern design of the Apple Store to the box that contains your computer or your iPad, everything you see or touch is designed to enhance your experience with the brand.

## CAUTION: Packaging Will Not Overcome Understanding Deficiencies in the Marketplace

Referring back again to "My Failed Experience as an Entrepreneur," part of my failure was as a result of too much time worrying about packaging—how my business cards and stationary would look, as well as the CD cover and the booklet inside—instead of researching the viability of the true market demand.

Because I had worked with Lee Clow for 21 years, the world-famous Creative Director at Chiat/Day, I asked him to design my business cards and stationary. If I had to pay him for these services, I would have had the most expensive cards in the history of the world. But fortunately for me, Lee agreed to help me at no charge.

I thought I was good to go. My packaging was top-notch, my value equation was pretty good, and my distribution system (Amazon) was adequate. Unfortunatty, great packaging could not compensate for my basic business problem. I simply could not attract enough people to buy my CD to make it a viable business. I didn't understand that the CD itself, without the additional element of live performances, was not enough to attract a large enough audience or market.

The subject of packaging comes up all the time with my SCORE clients. They ask me if I like their logo or their name or their website design. I try to tell them that these are important elements, but not nearly as important as the following basic questions:

- Who is going to buy this product?
- Why would they buy it versus the competition?
- How many do you have to sell to break even?

Understandably, we have a lot more fun being creative rather than tackling the really important, albeit difficult issues facing our business. So, pay attention to the packaging, but remember, great packaging alone will not make your business successful.

## STRATEGY #3: Be More Convenient (Distribution/Place)

Being more convenient by expanding your distribution is one of the most important strategies for business growth, an obvious example being, of course, Starbucks. The primary tool for business growth for Starbucks was to open  more stores. At the peak of their distribution outreach they had stores facing stores on opposite sides of the street. Expanding distribution also meant opening stores in other countries. Now, Starbucks has locations in every major city around the world. It has become truly global.

In our lifetime there has been one technology that has seriously revolutionized the concept of distribution— the Internet. With the Internet, any business can literally expand distribution worldwide without building a single office structure or hiring one employee. The Internet has made it possible for a small-town guitar teacher to reach everyone in the world who has an online connection.

The other major revolution in distribution is Amazon. Now, anyone can get their products sold, shipped, and delivered to virtually any place in the world.

As exciting as these technologies are, we should not overlook the more mundane, but important examples of how businesses have made it more convenient for consumers.

It's easy to list the major ways in which businesses, from banks to fast-food outlets, have made it more convenient for customers, with drive-up windows, delivery service, longer hours of operation, and the invention of the ATM. The youth today cannot conceive that when I was young you had to go into a bank and wait in long lines to get a check cashed. What made it worse was that the banks were only open Monday through Friday from 9:00 a.m. to 3:00 p.m. when most people were at work.

A good way to think about distribution for your business is to ask yourself, "How can I make it easier for people to buy my products or services?" This is especially true on the Internet. Look at the way Amazon has reduced the number of clicks to purchase an item. Amazon and Zappos both have figured out how to deliver books, shoes, and almost anything else to your door within days. Up next, rumor has it that Amazon is currently testing "same-day service."

Other examples of expanded distribution follow:

• Apple opens retail stores.

• Nissan creates a separate brand and a new distribution system called Infiniti to reach a more upscale market.

• Chiat/Day Advertising opens offices in seven cities across the country to service Nissan Dealers.

• Wolfgang Puck opens Wolfgang Puck Express restaurants in airport terminals and in metro areas to provide fast sit-down service.

• Pizza Hut begins delivery service.

• SCORE 114 operates seminars and workshops in libraries around the Orange County area.

## STRATEGY #4: Create a Better Value (Price)

In my seminars, I always say that most businesses spend too much time thinking about price and not enough on value.

Oscar Wilde once said, "People know the price of everything, but the value of nothing." [10]

First off, price is the amount of money someone pays for a product or service. It's simply a number. It's static; the ultimate logical reality. If the price is $10, it's the same for everyone.

Value, on the other hand, is not about quantity but quality. Value is a way of quantifying what is important to us individually. How important or valuable is this product or service to us at a given moment in time? As I have already pointed out, value is basically an equation: Value = Benefits Divided by Cost.

In this equation there are two ways you can increase the value: You can either reduce the price or enhance the benefits. But first, you must learn about the concept of value.

The most important thing to understand is that we all possess different values. Furthermore, the same person can sometimes value different things at different times. For example, when we are impatient or in a hurry, we value speed. When we are trying to sleep, we value quiet.

One of my SCORE colleagues, named Bill, values cheap gas. He will drive out of his way to save money when fueling up. As for me, I do not care what

10  Oscar Wilde, "The Picture of Dorian Gray"

gasoline costs because I hardly put any miles on my car (16,000 in four years.) Even though Bill tries to save money on gas, it does not mean he is cheap. He will willingly pay $30 to $100 for a good bottle of wine. I, on the other hand, am perfectly happy with "Two Buck Chuck." Bill values cheap gas; I value cheap wine.

The following are obvious examples of how some people may be willing to pay more for things they value:

• Even though the initial purchase price of a Mercedes Benz is high, some may say it is a better value because it historically has done a good job of holding its worth when it comes time to sell or trade it in on a new model.

• A person with a family may be willing to pay a premium for a Volvo because he or she believes it will keep their children safer than other cars.

• A divorced, wealthy, middle-aged man could pay a very high price for a Ferrari because he is convinced it will give him the benefits of speed, sex, and status.

• A couple might pay a higher price for a house because they want their children to attend a school in a certain school district.

• Yet another homebuyer may not object to paying more for property with an ocean view.

In marketing, one of the ways of increasing the value of something is by the use of Positioning. (I highly recommend the book, *Positioning*, by Trout and Ries, listed in my bibliography.) In everyday English, positioning simply defines how we compare things to one another.

At Chiat/Day, when we introduced the new Altima, we decided not to compare it with the Honda Accord and the Toyota Camry, but rather with the more expensive Lexus. We then developed the brilliant tagline, "Affordable Luxury."

Southwest Airlines has done a great job of increasing their value with their campaign, "Bags Fly Free." Instead of lowering their prices, Southwest has created a wonderful benefit that none of their competitors offer. No one likes to pay extra for bags.

Several years ago, when Hyundai was first introduced in the U.S. market, they sold a lot of cars, but they had real problems with reliability. In response, Hyundai came out with the best warranty in the business. This was a terrific way to increase their value equation.

Regent Cruise Lines created a loyalty program in which customers who spent more than 200 nights on their ships were granted Platinum Status. Two of the major benefits of being Platinum, in addition to early boarding and other niceties, were free laundry and Internet Service, which can get pretty pricey away from port.

Unfortunately, as everyone knows, the easiest and quickest way to improve the value equation is simply to reduce the price. Generally, I advise my clients not to take this route unless they want to end up like the airline industry or worse yet, General Motors. However, there are instances where businesses have used reduced pricing effectively, one being the Nordstrom Semi-Annual Sale.

The following is a list of simple things any business can do to improve its value equation:

- Offer a money-back guarantee
- Include shipping at no additional cost

- Create a Value-Pack (like a hamburger, fries and a drink)

## STRATEGY #5: Be Better Known (Promotion)

Purchase Funnel

Finally, we come to the place that most people think is really marketing: promotion, advertising, and public relations. When I talk with small-business owners who tell me they have a marketing problem, usually what they mean is that they are not able to generate enough awareness.

There is little doubt that the easiest, quickest, and surest way of generating awareness is to buy advertising. I know something about this business because I spent over 21 years of my career in an advertising agency where we helped our clients spend enormous amounts of money.

If you have millions of dollars to spend on a television commercial that runs during the Super Bowl or the Academy Awards or any other highly rated TV show, you can be reasonably certain that you will generate awareness.

Even with all the excitement about the Internet, television is still the proven winner in generating awareness quickly to the broadest possible audience. But for virtually all of the people I mentor and counsel, television and other paid media are really not options. They simply do not have the budget.

If you don't have the money to buy awareness then you need some combination of talent, luck, or skill. If you are a singer and you can get on "American Idol" like Kelly Clarkson, then you can achieve almost overnight awareness and celebrity status. If you have a new product for the home and you go to a major trade show—take for instance, The Housewares Convention in Chicago—you can get your product on the Today Show as one of my clients did. If you have unique, beautiful handbags and you know somebody who knows somebody, you can gain exposure on the Oprah Winfrey Show, as my client, Laga Bags did. But, these opportunities are rare and unpredictable.

Lacking money, the very best way to increase awareness for your business is through publicity, which means that someone else writes or talks about your business or demonstrates your product to the public. The trick here is to convince that certain someone to actually want to write or talk about your business in a magazine, newspaper, or on television. The only reason they will want to do that is because they believe your product or service will be 1) interesting, 2) entertaining, and/or 3) useful to their audience.

One of my favorite examples of generating awareness is a company called LifeLock that used the very same strategy Apple used to introduce the Macintosh Computer in 1984—buying a television commercial on the Super Bowl that generated hundreds of millions of dollars in free publicity.

What's interesting about the LifeLock story is that they played up the greatest fear people have since the inception of Internet sales—identity theft. To convince consumers to buy their identity-protection service they purchased a couple of mobile billboards to drive around the clogged streets of Manhattan with the following message printed in giant letters:

"My Social Security Number is 570-00-0000. I am so confident I can protect you that I am willing to give out my social security number to everyone."

LifeLock also bought a full-page ad in the New York Times with the same message. For a relatively small amount of media money, LifeLock was able to get literally millions of dollars' worth of publicity. Every major news outlet picked up this story, and in a period of two or three weeks, LifeLock went from relative obscurity to becoming a household word.

Even though this example took some cash, I would argue that the real essence of the success of this campaign was the idea itself, which didn't cost a cent. The idea to give out the CEO's social security number was ridiculous, but this fact alone is what made it brilliant. Because it was outrageous, it was news. It was a human-interest story. If you want to get publicity, you need a story to which everyone can relate. That is the bottom line.

Press releases, on the other hand, are all about us. The press release is the most selfish and solipsistic form of communication known to man. It is all about how great "we" are. "We are the X Company and we have just introduced the new blah, blah, blah." Realistically, nobody cares. That is why unless you have something equivalent to a cure for cancer, your press release will most likely get thrown into the trash.

Of course, it is also possible to generate awareness all on your own on the Internet. If you can create a video that goes viral (like Dave Carroll did with "United Breaks Guitars"), you can reach hundreds of millions of people in a very short amount of time.

## INTERNET SEARCH

Some of you may want to know how you can get your company to come up on Page One of a Google Search. One way is to buy your way on. These paid positions are the ones you see at the top of the Google search page with the beige backgrounds.

The only other ways are 1) either to be the most widely used company associated with a particular product, i.e., Amazon = Books, or 2) master the complexities and ever-changing realities of Search Engine Optimization (SEO).

I will be the first to admit that I am unqualified to speak about how to optimize your website for a Google search. However, what I can tell you is that while it is possible to get a lot of hits by maximizing SEO, you might discover later that as much as 80% to 90% of traffic actually comes to your site by accident. In other words, when they reach your website they may realize that you are not what they were really looking for.

## CAUTION: Awareness is Not the Holy Grail

If the dot.com crash taught us anything, it is that awareness by itself is not enough to make a company successful.

Guy Kawasaki, bestselling author and former Apple employee, talks about the downfall of PetFood.com in one of his videos. PetFood.com ran commercials during the Super Bowl where they had incredibly high awareness, yet it failed because the basic business model itself was flawed.

## KNOWN FOR WHAT

The final point about being "Better Known" is that it's relatively easy to be known if you don't care about the reason why. Most people on the planet have heard of Santa Claus and Hitler, two personalities on opposite ends of the good and evil spectrum. However, this is a perfect example of why good marketing is not just about generating awareness. It is about creating positive perception. If you want your business or brand to be known for something positive like Santa Claus, you have to stand for something positive. Equally important, you must behave and perform in a way that everyone will perceive as positive, which means you have to be known for satisfying customers' needs, wants, and desires.

## SUMMARY

Hopefully, the previous examples of "The Big 5" gave you a glimpse of proven strategies that you can use to grow your business. In every example, from satisfying more needs and wants to making their products and services more attractive, accessible, and valuable, these ideas were free. It didn't take money. It took someone who was willing to think about something in a new, creative, out-of-the-box way. It took imaginative ideas.

# MARKETING LEVERAGE

## *How You Can Use*
## *"The Big 5" to Grow Your Business*

Now that we have looked at several examples of how other companies have used "The Big 5" strategies to grow their businesses, it is time for you to go to work and put everything you have learned into a coherent plan to increase your business growth. Let's examine some specific ways that you can utilize these strategies.

### STRATEGY #1: Solve More Consumer Needs/Wants

Instead of asking yourself, "What am I selling?" start with, "What is the customer really buying?"

| You Are Selling | Customer Is Buying |
| --- | --- |
| Mercedes Benz Automobiles | Distinctive, Stylish Transportation |
| Gym Memberships | Better Physical Shape/Fitness |
| Apple iPod | More Convenient Way to Carry Music Around |

As a small-business owner, you need to think about how you can solve more problems for your customers, because the more problems you solve and the more needs you can satisfy, the more money customers will give you.

The reality is that many times business success comes not from inventing an entirely new product, but simply by improving upon something that already exists. The iPod is really just a better version of an MP3, which proves the old adage of building a better mousetrap.

One of my favorite business stories about solving people's needs is the invention of Post-it Notes by 3M. Talk about serving needs. Before the Post-it Note, people would scribble down notes on a scrap of paper, then use scotch tape to stick it to something as a reminder. One day, some brilliant person at 3M asked, "Why not create a new product that combines these two needs into one?"

For Laga Bags, the answer to how they could meet more customer needs was to create a new product. In addition to selling beautiful, artistic handbags, Roy and Louise figured they could meet more needs by creating artistic sleeves to hold iPads, which they now sell hundreds of every month.

Another one of my clients, Ben Golsha, sells used cars out of his business, "Auto Bazaar." I asked Ben, "Who are these people coming in to buy a used car? What are their needs?" We discussed the idea that many of his potential customers did not have transportation to get to his car lot. So he implemented a pick-up service to deliver them to his location.

In order to solve more of your customers' needs and wants, you must ask yourself the following questions:

- What products or services am I currently selling?
- What needs do these products or services currently satisfy?
- What new needs could I serve?
- What other customer problems could I solve?
- How could I be more helpful?

## STRATEGY #2: Be More Attractive

Just as in "The Attraction Game" in Chapter 3, it is time for you to think about how you can make your business more attractive. What can you do to enhance everything that people see about your business?

How can you make your business cards more interesting? Maybe you don't even need cards. Remember my client, Chris, the window cleaner, who instead gives out ballpoint pens with his name and phone number?

How can you make your invoices more attractive and interesting? What if you added a note reminding customers about how you exceeded their expectations? What if you asked your customers to tell you what other needs or wants your business might solve?

Do you have a website? What can you do to improve it? Of course, if you are trying to improve your site, the first questions you need to ask are, "What is the purpose of your website? What do you want people to do?" Make sure that your website is focused on this single objective. If you want the phone to ring, make sure that everything is about getting the prospective customer to make a phone call. If you want to sell something, make it uncomplicated for the person to purchase your product or service.

While we are on the subject of packaging, some products seem to go out of their way to be less user-friendly and attractive. One of the things I really don't like is the vacuum-packed shrink wrap that some companies have used to deter theft. Many times I wonder if the people who sell these items have ever actually tried to open up one of their packages. I now carry around a massive pair of scissors just to cut these offensive plastic cocoons. This is an example of how to make your product less convenient and friendly.

If you have an office or a retail store, what can you do to make it more attractive?

Also, remember when we played "The Attraction Game", the importance of asking, "Attractive to whom?" The type of bait you use will determine what kind of fish you catch. Are you making yourself attractive to the right people? What can I do to make my products or services more functional and useful to my desired customer?

Sometimes, asking these questions can be a great reason to interact with your customers. When I was designing the cover for this book, I asked the people on my Facebook page and in an email blast to tell me which of two cover designs they liked better. I got some great comments and it really helped me make a final decision.

## STRATEGY #3: Be More Convenient

The question you need to ask in terms of this strategy is, "How can I make it easier and more convenient for my customers to buy my product or service?"

Obviously, one of the best ways to expand your distribution system and make things more convenient in today's world is to use the world-wide-web. Nowadays, a guitar teacher in a small town with an Internet connection can easily serve customers anywhere on the globe.

One of the best examples of a business making their product more accessible is the way the U.S. Postal Service has made buying stamps more convenient. Nothing used to be more painful than going to the post office and waiting in long lines. Now stamps are for sale in vending machines, on the Internet, at the grocery store, and in several retail outlets. If the U.S. Postal Service can figure out how to be more convenient, so can you.

Another way to improve your business is to ask people what they don't like about your product or service.

Sometimes, you can't exactly solve these issues, but you can learn a great deal from them. Regent Cruise Lines learned two things their customers did not like by following this strategy: 1) paying for Internet service, and 2) the limited availability of washing machines and dryers. They solved these issues by providing free Internet and laundry service to customers who had spent more than 200 nights on their ships.

Lastly, how and where can consumers currently buy your products or services? How about increasing the hours your store is open? What if you opened another location? Can you offer delivery service?

## STRATEGY #4: Create A Better Value

The goal of marketing is to focus on value, not price. If you have been paying attention, by now you should be familiar with the following value equation:

$$\text{Value} = \frac{\text{Benefits}}{\text{Cost}}$$

This is a handy equation because it reminds us that there are only two ways to increase the value of an item: 1) you can increase the benefits or 2) you can decrease the price.

Almost everything has a price. "Free" simply means that you do not have to pay any money, but there are usually still costs involved. For example, to get to a free SCORE seminar you have to get out of your recliner and leave the warmth and comfort of your home. Then you have to drive the distance to the location of the seminar, not to mention pay the high cost of gasoline. Plus, your time involved is worth something, isn't it? So, even though the seminar is free, there is a cost to attend.

It is always tempting for small businesses to want to reduce the price as a way of improving the value equation. According to the latest research, slightly more than one-third of the consumer population considers low price to be the most important factor in their decision to purchase. These are the people who shop regularly at Walmart and other discount stores.

However, it is very difficult for a small-business owner to compete with Walmart and other discount retailers on price. One of the reasons these big-box retailers can offer such low prices is because of the tremendous volume in which they order and, as a result, can buy for less. My advice to small-business owners is, unless you can buy things for less than Walmart, do not compete on price. The big retailers will simply put you out of business.

Sometimes my clients ask, "Is it ever okay to put my merchandise on sale?" Of course you can. But make sure that it is perceived to be just a special limited offer. Nordstrom has a very effective sale twice a year. They have trained their customers to understand that the sale will definitely end on a certain date, unlike car companies that just run one sale after another.

The lesson here is that if you are going to have a sale, make sure your customers know that this is not a permanent re-pricing of your merchandise. I know this takes discipline, but the alternative is ugly.

So, how can you increase the benefits of your product or service? If roughly one-third of consumers agree that low price is the most important reason to purchase one item over another, what about the remaining two-thirds?

Porsche automobiles, first-class airline seats, deluxe suites on cruise ships, box seats at baseball games, etc.—these are just a few examples of things that are not purchased because of low cost. In fact, almost two-thirds (65%) of all purchase decisions are based on consumers' desire for quality products or better service, not the lowest price.

There are, in fact, two good ways to increase your value equation without reducing your price: 1) You can improve the quality and performance of your products, or 2) you can improve the level of service.

In the last few decades we have seen that the two most successful kinds of businesses have been those at the top and the bottom of the market. High-end stores like Tiffany's, Nordstrom, and Apple have done very well, as have low-end stores such as Costco, Walmart, and Target. The ones that have done less well, and in some cases have gone out of business, are the stores in the middle. The problem is that these "middle stores" attract neither the person who wants the lowest price nor the person who wants the best quality and/or service. If you want good quality and good service, you shop at Nordstrom. If you want the lowest price, you shop at the discount stores. If you are in the middle, who needs to shop there?

We see examples of this all around us. On most cruise ships, the first two categories of cabins to sell out are the least expensive (those usually at the bottom of the ship, interior cabins with no windows to the outside world) and the most expensive deluxe suites (usually at the top of the ship.) The cabins in the middle are the last to sell out.

The reality is that if you can't be the cheapest, you have to be the best, or at least better than your competition in some specific way. A good way to think about this is to consider all of the various dimensions and manifestations of the two words–quality and service.

The following are examples of specific elements of both the "Quality" and "Service" components:

| Quality | Service |
|---|---|
| Reliability | Convenience |
| The way it feels, smells, and looks | Fast |
| Performance (speed, handling, power) | Hassle-free |
| Workmanship | Luxury |
| Cleanliness | Easy to Use |
| Safety | Nice/Friendly |
| It helps me to do something better | Trustworthy/Honesty/Accurate/ Thoroughness/Helpful |

I am sure you can think of many more components that I have not listed here. But basically, in order to increase your value equation or become more valuable to customers, you need to figure out how you can exceed expectations in at least one of these dimensions.

The bottom line about the value equation is that you have to make your business or your brand more valuable to someone. Think about what products and services are valuable to you? Most likely, it is because in some way they make your life better—more comfortable, convenient, interesting, or satisfying. These products or services fulfill some rational or emotional need in your life that makes you feel better.

The question you need to ask now is, "How can I make my business more valuable to my customers?"

## STRATEGY #5: Be Better Known

Finally, how can you make your business, your brand, and your products better known in the marketplace? The answer is easy. You need to generate awareness and move prospective customers down the Purchase Funnel.

As I mentioned earlier, for the small-business person with a very limited or nonexistent budget for paid media, you need to generate awareness via publicity: getting articles written about you in newspapers/magazines; getting on popular TV shows like Oprah Winfrey's former show or the Today Show, etc.; or by positive word-of-mouth either using social media or from customer referrals.

I have had clients whose products were featured on both the Oprah Winfrey Show and the Today Show and I can tell you that the results were spectacular. When Laga Bags were featured on Oprah, sales literally went through the roof. This kind of publicity is invaluable. The only negative is that it is totally unpredictable. So, you can't plan your business around it.

I had another SCORE client who got their product on the Today Show. Unfortunately, the program aired before the company was able to produce in mass quantity so they were not able to capitalize on this great publicity. What a lost opportunity!

## SUMMARY

In Part I of Chapter 6, I showed you how other companies like Apple, Starbucks, Chiat/Day, and Wolfgang Puck Food Company used "The Big 5" to grow their businesses. Using these same strategies in your business will also help you achieve the greatest leverage and the highest return on your investment of time, money, and energy. If you concentrate your energies and efforts on improving your ability to master these five strategies, I can guarantee your business will grow dramatically.

Now, you get a chance to participate. Fill in the chart on the next page for your business using the questions below the chart as a guide.

| "The Big 5" | How Can I Implement This Strategy in My Business? |
|---|---|
| Solve More Consumer Needs/Wants: | |
| Be More Attractive: | |
| Be More Convenient: | |
| Create a Better Value: | |
| Be Better Known: | |

The following are questions you can answer to help you with each of the above strategies:

## SOLVE MORE CONSUMER NEEDS/WANTS

• What other customer needs or wants can you satisfy in your business?

• What new products or services can you provide to your customers that would make you more valuable to them and more loyal to your business?

## BE MORE ATTRACTIVE

• What can you do to make everything that people see about your business (from stationary to storefront to website) more interesting, more attractive, or more functional for your customers?

## BE MORE CONVENIENT

• How can you make it more convenient for your customers to buy your products or services?

• How can you make your products or services more accessible to customers? (Longer hours, more days of the week, more locations, free shipping, etc.)

## CREATE A BETTER VALUE

• How can you increase your perceived quality or service?

• How can you increase the benefits you provide to your customers?

• How can you be better than your competitors in one or two dimensions of quality (performance, safer, cleaner, more dependable) or service (faster, more convenient, easy to use, nicer, friendlier, more honest, trustworthy)?

## BE BETTER KNOWN

• How can you generate awareness through paid media or free publicity, word-of-mouth, or social media?

• How can you move your customers down the Purchase Funnel? (See Chapter 11 for more on this subject.)

# HOW TO SELECT THE RIGHT TARGET AUDIENCE

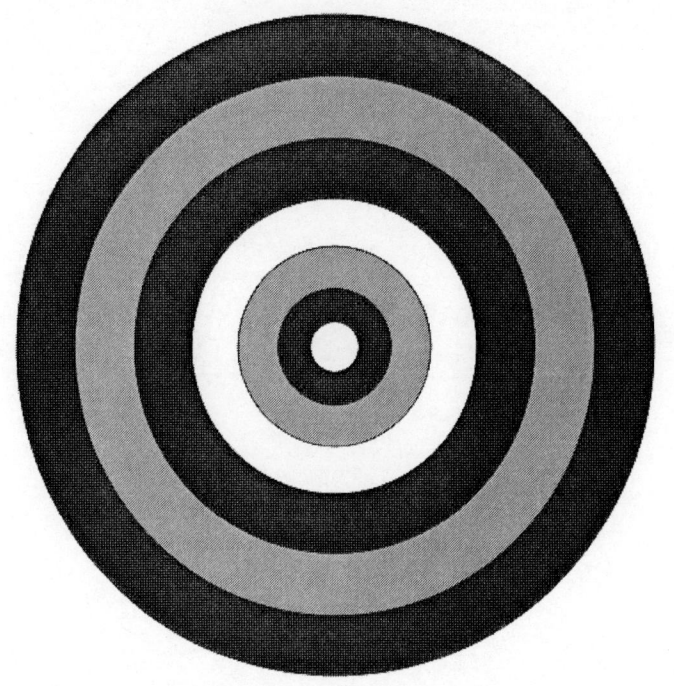

# Chapter 7

# HOW TO SELECT THE RIGHT TARGET AUDIENCE

Marketing is defined as "everything you do to attract and retain customers." This is a key element in *Marketing Without Money*. So, what kind of customers do you want to attract and retain?

There's no pressure here, take your time. But promise me that you'll really think about this because your answer determines everything else you do in marketing.

When we talk about your target audience, we are simply asking, "Attractive to whom?" In other words, "Who is the most likely prospect to buy your products or services?"

## THE WRONG ANSWER

Many times, people answer without thinking by saying "Everyone" and to be honest, I do understand their train of thought. They figure, "Why shouldn't I try to reach the largest possible audience?" Well, I'll tell you. One good reason you should not include everyone in your target audience is because it is a waste of your time and money, two things of which a small business has limited amounts.

In my career, I have had numerous discussions with top executives who wanted to believe that everyone in the world is potentially their target audience. Basically, their argument was, "Well, they might not buy our product today, but maybe someday in the future they will buy it." Suffice it to say, I am not a fan of the "maybe someday" strategy, especially for the small-business owner.

Another important aspect of defining your target audience is to understand the difference between being "effective" and "efficient." Television commercials can be extremely effective, but they are not very efficient. Television by nature is not an especially targeted medium. When I worked on the Nissan account at Chiat/Day, our target for TV was "Adults, 18-34." That's not a precise target. It is like a golfer who hits his shot from the tee and says his target is "anywhere on the grass."

One of the most important messages in *Marketing Without Money* is to get you to stop wasting time and money by trying to sell your products or services to people who are not likely to buy them.

## HOW TO DEFINE YOUR TARGET AUDIENCE

The usual way people begin to define their target audience is by demographics. For example, young men, working women, teens, etc.

Having helped many small-business owners define the most likely person to buy their product, I prefer to take a different approach. I am more interested in behavior than demographics. I want to know what these people do. I want to know what behavior of theirs is important to my business. Generally, the most significant element of their behavior is that these people buy something.

The next part of behavior I'm curious about has to do with quantity or frequency of their buying behavior. How much do they buy or how often?

Finally, and most importantly, I want to know what these people value. What is important to them?

In dealing with an automotive client like Nissan, here's how this approach would work.

1. Q: What does Nissan's target audience do?

   A: They buy new cars. More specifically, they buy new import-branded cars.

2. Q: How frequently do they buy?

   A: They buy every three to five years.

3. Q: What do they value?

   A: They value quality and reliability.

Using this example as a template, we will go through the process for other kinds of businesses. Let's start by figuring out the target audience for Chiat/Day Advertising Agency.

1. Q: What does Chiat/Day's target audience do?

   A: They buy advertising.

We could get even more specific and ask, "What kinds of organizations buy advertising?" The answer is organizations with budgets for advertising and marketing.

Honing it down even further, we want to know the specific person within the organization that is our target audience. "What person(s) in what position in these organizations is likely to have control of a marketing or advertising budget?" The answer in most organizations is the CEO, the Marketing Manager, or maybe the Advertising Manager.

Now we are getting closer to articulating who the target audience is for Chiat/Day Advertising. Once we know who the most likely prospect is to hire an advertising agency, we can figure out how to be more attractive to this target and we can determine who needs to be aware of Chiat/Day.

Based on this process, we can conclude that the target audience for Chiat/Day is a CEO or Marketing Manager who has control of an advertising budget.

But now we need to get even more targeted. Now that we know they buy advertising, we need to know the frequency or quantity in which they buy. In other words, what is the amount of advertising they can afford or what is the size of their advertising budget?

When I retired from Chiat/Day in 1998, it had been acquired by Omnicom and merged with another agency, TBWA. Our annual revenues were more than $100 million. We were no longer the small boutique agency I went to work for in 1977. We were dealing with big clients and big budgets. So we really weren't set up for, nor were we very interested in clients with an advertising budget of less than say $25 million.

2.  Q: In what quantity do they buy?

   A: The CEO or Marketing Manager has control of an advertising budget greater than $25 million.

Using another golf analogy, we are now on the green. We are getting closer to the hole by making our target smaller and more precise.

But there is one more piece to the puzzle, and quite frankly, the single most important. We know that our target prospect buys advertising and that they buy more than $25 million a year. Now, we need to know what they value.

Chiat/Day had a reputation for producing breakthrough advertising—daring, outrageous, and edgy commercials like the "1984" spot for Apple, the Taco Bell Chihuahua and the Energizer Bunny campaigns. But for some business owners, breakthrough means risky. What if people don't like it? What if we offend someone? Why don't we show more of the product? Why isn't the logo bigger? In fact, out of all of the companies with large advertising budgets, there was, and probably still is, only a small percentage that would really want and value breakthrough advertising. The proof for this belief is all the boring, dull, and silly television commercials we see every day.

3.  Q: What do they value?

    A: The CEO or a Marketing Manager who has control of an advertising budget greater than $25 million, values breakthrough advertising.

Notice that the description of the target audience for Chiat/Day Advertising Agency has three parts:

1.  Who is it? (the CEO or Marketing Director)

2.  A level of quantification (at least $25 million advertising budget)

3.  A statement of what they value (Breakthrough advertising)

Let's demonstrate another example. Who is the target audience for SCORE? When I first became a volunteer for SCORE in 2002, the people in our chapter believed that their target was small-business owners. I was not satisfied with this answer. I thought it was too big, too imprecise. So I went through my three-question approach.

1.  Q: What does SCORE's target audience do?

    A: They seek help and advice.

Already I have narrowed the target. With 30 years of marketing experience I can tell you unequivocally that not everyone seeks advice. Many of the clients I dealt with at Chiat/Day believed they already knew everything. There are also a number of small-business owners who are not seeking help. Maybe they feel they are too busy or they distrust outside advice. Whatever the reason, they do not want guidance.

In this particular case, the question of frequency or quantity is probably irrelevant. So we can go directly to the third question, "What do they value?"

After 10 years of volunteering as a SCORE counselor, I can tell you that SCORE clients value experience and expertise. When I let my clients know that I have dealt with successful companies such as Nike, Apple, and other major brands like Nissan and Pizza Hut, they figure I must know something.

The other thing that SCORE clients value and appreciate is the integrity of our motive. We are not trying to sell anything. We want to help. I wrestled with this issue when it came to publishing this book. How could I maintain the integrity of not trying to sell something, but rather, just wanting to help? My solution was to donate all of my net proceeds to the SCORE foundation. My goal is not to make money. I am trying to help people be better marketers.

3. Q: What do they value?

A: Small-business owners who seek help and advice, value expertise, integrity of motive, and free counseling.

In my seminars, I ask the audience to participate in defining a target audience for different products by having them pretend they are the Marketing Director for a beer company.

As a Marketing Director for a beer company you must ask, "What does your target do that is important for you to know?" Of course, the first answer I get is, "They drink beer," which is wrong. I use this example because it helps demonstrate how important it is to think critically about this question.

The correct answer, at least to me is, "They buy beer." The distinction between people who drink beer and those who buy beer is important. I inform my audience that when I went to college, it was almost never necessary to buy beer. You could get it at every fraternity and sorority party within a half mile of the campus. I once argued, in jest, that if you bought beer you weren't smart enough to be in college.

1.  Q: What do they do?

A: They buy beer.

To see how important the distinction between drinking and buying beer is, let's look at Google or Facebook, which emphasizes the fact that there is a huge difference between a user and a customer. I am a user of Google, but I am not their customer. Google does not receive any money from me. The target customer for

Google is the advertiser. Therefore, my definition of the customer or client is "someone who pays you."

In this case, the second question regarding quantity or frequency is very important. It is obvious that a person who buys two cases of beer a week is a much better customer than one who buys a six-pack a month. So let's arbitrarily define our target as a person who buys at least one six-pack a week.

2.   Q: How frequently do they buy?

A: They buy at least one six-pack a week.

Now we need to talk about what these beer buyers value. Like all of us, people who drink beer value different things. Some value low price, some want to drink a lot of beer without getting filled up (remember the campaign for Lite Beer "Great Taste/Less Filling"), and others value unique home brew, etc. In today's market, Michelob Light Beer has a different approach. Their campaign is all about calories. The values have shifted from wanting to drink more to desiring fewer calories.

Let's finish the assignment for the Marketing Director of a beer company by getting even more specific. Let's say this is the Marketing Director for Michelob Light.

3.   Q: What do they value?

A: They are concerned with calorie consumption.

Now that we have done a couple of these exercises, let's make it a bit more complicated and challenging.

Let's try to define the target audience for Wolfgang Puck Food Company when we introduced our first product, frozen apple tarts. The customer for WPFC was not the end user, but rather the retailer, or in this case, the supermarket. I will repeat. The customer for WPFC was the buyer at the supermarket, because the retailer was the entity who paid us for our frozen tarts.

1.   Q: What do they do?

A: The supermarket buyer buys products to fill their shelves.

2.   Q: How frequently do they buy?

A: They buy several cases a week.

The most important question here is, "What do they value?" It did not take me very long to learn what buyers in supermarkets care about. They consider how many cases they can sell and what margin they will make. Supermarket buyers care about case volume and profit margin.

This specific information told us at WPFC what we had to do to get a buyer interested in our product. We had to have a track record demonstrating that our product would sell in sufficient quantity and with good margins.

There is another component that is also important to supermarket buyers. They want to put products on their shelves that correspond to the wishes and desires of their actual consumers.

This point was made clear to me one day when my wife sent me to Gelson's Market to pick up some Hamburger Helper. When I could not find it on the shelves, I went to the manager and asked where it was located. Without taking a breath, he responded, "That's not our customer. We don't carry that."

3.  Q: What do they value?

A: They want maximum volume and good profit margins from a product that will be compatible with their customers' wants and needs.

## SUMMARY

To identify your best target customer or client you must ask the following three questions:

1.  What does your target audience do that is relative to your product or service?

The key word in this sentence is "do." What does he or she do? This is a verb, an action. Beer customers buy beer; Chiat/Day clients buy advertising.

Fill in the blank:

"My target audience buys _____."

2.  How often (frequency) or how much (quantity) does your target audience buy?

Remember, we don't want all customers, just good and great customers.

3.  What does your target audience value?

This is the most important and often most neglected part of the target audience description.

Remember, at Chiat/Day we were selling breakthrough advertising. Nike sells products to people who value athletic performance. Volvo sells cars to families who value safety. Apple sells to people who want easy to use, great looking, and cool products. SCORE wants clients who seek advice and value integrity of motive.

Getting a handle on what your customers really value is a critical part of becoming a good marketer. To know what someone values is to know how you can please them, or at least not disappoint them.

If you know someone who values promptness, you shouldn't be late for an appointment. If a person values honesty, don't lie to them. If someone's top priority is neatness and cleanliness, clean up your house or your apartment.

The interesting thing about values is that they are a shifting sea. There are very few absolute values. We all have a core set, but within that, our values change depending on our specific needs and demands. Sometimes we want a deal, other times we want the best. If we're in a hurry, we want fast food, but when we're with friends or family, we want to spend a leisurely time enjoying good food and conversation.

If you are married or have a significant other, you probably know what he or she values. You are aware of this because over time you have observed his or her behavior. You have seen them when they get upset. You know when they are pleased. Understanding values is mainly about paying attention and asking the right questions.

## TARGETING: A Real World Example

The recent 2012 Presidential Election provides an interesting example of the importance of focusing on the right target. An enormous amount of money ($2 billion+) was spent by both candidates, Barak Obama and Mitt Romney.

But from a marketing perspective, more interesting than all the money spent, was the way the two campaigns targeted their messages to niche segments or micro-targets of the electorate. If you were a member of the NRA, you got one message. If you attended church on a regular basis, your message was different. If you were for same-sex marriage, yet another was delivered. Both campaigns relied upon precise data about how people behaved and with what special interest groups they were affiliated.

Most of us know how difficult it is to persuade someone to switch his or her vote. The people who run the campaigns know this too. That is why they do not waste their money trying to get Democrats to vote Republican or vice versa. Instead, the campaigns spend the majority of their advertising budgets talking to their base and trying to influence those described as Independent voters.

If we were to translate this into our marketing Purchase Process or the Purchase Funnel, Independent voters would be those who are in the CONSIDER phase. They are AWARE of both candidates and they would CONSIDER voting for either one. The campaign manager's job is to move them down through the Purchase Funnel from CONSIDER to INTEND to the final phase, VOTE.

Let's pretend that you are working for Romney's presidential campaign. How would you go about defining your target audience?

A lot of people have very strong opinions about poli-tics, but not all of them actually vote. In fact, almost half of the eligible population does not show up at the polls on election day. So you must first identify registered voters and those who have voted in the past.

The next most important thing is to find out with which party they are affiliated. Are they registered as a Democrat, a Republican, or an Independent?

If you were working for the Republican campaign, you would want to target registered Republican or Independent voters. You would not waste your money on trying to persuade Democrats to vote for your candidate.

1.   Q: What do they do?

A: They vote for Republicans or Independents.

This is where you want to see if a person has voted in the past several elections or do they sometimes sit it out. Did they vote in the primaries? Did they vote in the last presidential election?

2.   Q: How often do they vote?

A: They voted in the past several elections.

3.   Q: What do they value?

A: To be determined.

In presidential elections, as it is with most of the things we purchase, what we value plays a primary role in how we behave and how we make choices.

I recently read a very interesting book published in 2012 titled, *The Righteous Mind: Why Good People are Divided by Politics and Religion*, written by Jonathan Haidt. According to this author, "There are at least six psychological systems that comprise the universal foundations of the world's many moral matrices." [11]

---

11  Jonathan Haidt, "The Righteous Mind: Why Good People are Divided by Politics and Religion" (Your Coach In A Box 2013)

Basically, Haidt is saying that people care about the following issues when they are deciding their political affiliation:

- The Care/Harm Foundation
- The Liberty/Oppression Foundation
- The Fairness/Cheating Foundation
- The Loyalty/Betrayal Foundation
- The Authority/Subversion Foundation
- The Sanctity/Degradation Foundation

Haidt's thesis is that, depending upon where you stand on each of these continuums or dualities will determine whether you tend to be more liberal or conservative.

Without arguing about the merits or specifics of Haidt's thesis, I like the concept that we can measure what people care about, what's important to them, and that by knowing what a person values we can better determine how they will behave—whether it's voting for the President of the United States or buying a new pair of shoes.

I believe that in marketing, we have at least three different foundations that provide the same sort of matrices or continuums:

- High Price vs. Low Price
- High Quality vs. Lower Quality
- Better Service vs. Poor Service

At any given moment, on any given day, we all make decisions about what goods and services to purchase based on how we feel about each of these dimensions at that particular time. As a small-business owner, it is important for you to figure out what your target customer cares about because this will determine how they behave.

# SOMETIMES
# YOUR CLIENTS CHOOSE YOU

One of the most brilliant things my wife has ever said is, "You don't choose your friends. Your friends choose you." Over the years I have found this to be so true and profound.

In most cases, the same can be said for businesses and their target audience. "You don't choose your target. Your target chooses you."

In 2004, my SCORE Client, Roy van Broekhuizen, was sent by Saddleback Church to Ochi, Indonesia to help victims of the great tsunami disaster. While there, Roy discovered some women who were making beautiful woven baskets and bags.

Roy came back to the U.S., and after discussing it with his wife, Louise, they decided to start a company called Laga Bags to help create jobs and revenues for the victims of the tsunami.

Starting from nothing in 2004, Roy and Louise attended trade shows to look for distributors, and slowly but steadily their business grew. Within a few years they had several retailers and distributors, and revenues of more than $500,000.

Quite by accident, at one of the trade shows, they discovered a group of people called quilters. These quilters made things with their hands, generally bed quilts, but the big discovery for Roy and Louise was that here was a new target audience, people who loved their bags. The quilters chose Laga Bags because they valued the beautiful handwork and thought they were an exceptional value for the price.

Partly because of this discovery, Laga Bags has doubled its business and now does more than $1 million in annual sales.

## EXAMPLES OF TARGETING

### NIKE TARGET CUSTOMER

*People who value athletic performance and authenticity*

### SCORE TARGET CUSTOMER

*Small business owners who are seeking help and value integrity of motive*

### CHIAT/DAY TARGET CUSTOMER

*A CEO or Marketing Director with an advertising budget of $25 million who wants breakthrough advertising*

### WOLFGANG PUCK TARGET CUSTOMER (For Frozen Tarts)

*The Frozen Food Buyer in supermarkets who values case sales and high margins*

### MICHELOB LIGHT TARGET CUSTOMER

*People who buy at least a six-pack of beer or more a week, and care about calories*

# HOW TO USE YOUR BEST CUSTOMERS TO GROW YOUR BUSINESS

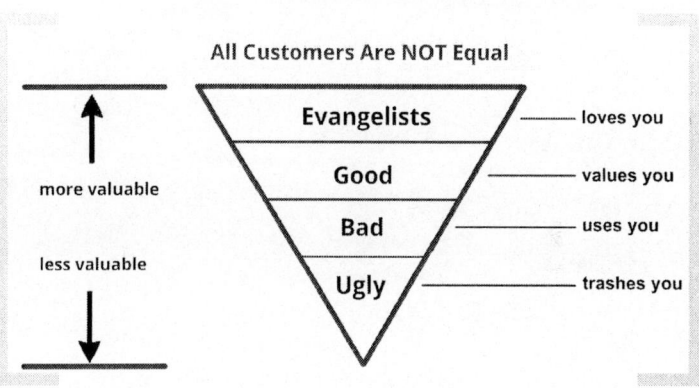

## Chapter 8

# HOW TO USE YOUR BEST CUSTOMERS TO GROW YOUR BUSINESS

## WHAT IS A CUSTOMER?

Since the primary role of a business is to create a customer, I should provide you with the definition of a customer, which is someone who pays you for your goods or services.

One hundred years ago, business was pretty simple. Someone made a pair of shoes and sold them to the person who needed the shoes. Nowadays, business is much more complex. Nissan Motors, USA, does not sell cars directly to the individuals who buy and drive cars. They sell to dealers who sell to individuals who drive their cars. Therefore, Nissan USA's customer/client is the Nissan dealer.

Even though the ultimate user is not, by my definition, a "customer" of Nissan Motors Corporation, the end user still needs to be included in the marketing communications. In the case of Nissan, millions of dollars were spent against the ultimate user to make them aware of new models and to try to persuade them to go into the dealers' showrooms. This is normal in a multi-tier distribution system. You may have to direct your marketing to users, as well as your customers.

## WHAT IS A GOOD CUSTOMER?

The goal of marketing is not to simply get more customers. The goal is to attract good customers to your business, then keep them satisfied for a long time. Good customers recognize and appreciate the value of your particular product or service and recommend it to their friends.

As a business owner, you are responsible for the kind of customers you attract. Just like fishing, the type of fish you catch will depend on the bait you use. If your bait is deals-and-discounts, you'll attract customers who want the lowest price. If your bait is quality-and-excellence, you will appeal to people who are willing to pay for the finer things in life.

## CUSTOMERS COME IN FOUR CATEGORIES

The goal in *Marketing Without Money* is not only to help you get more good and great customers, but also to reduce or eliminate the bad and the ugly. Something that may not be obvious to you yet, but will  be as you grow your business, is that customers come in four categories:

- Evangelists
- Good
- Bad
- Ugly

Let's begin at the bottom with the "Ugly" customer. First of all, this customer only buys your products or services when you have a deal. To make matters worse, they sometimes cause you persistent problems by either paying late or not at all, or they trash you, complaining about their bad experience. You do not need many of these customers to make your life miserable and send your business into bankruptcy.

Next up the ladder is the "Bad" customer. Like the "Ugly," this customer also only buys your products or services when you have a deal. However, they don't complain or criticize your business to others. They're just bargain shoppers, always looking for a way to save money. They take advantage of your discounts, but they really have no loyalty. They do not value you.

Next up the ladder is the "Good" customer who recognizes and appreciates the value of your products and services and is happy to pay you a fair price. The "Good" customer uses your products or services on a regular basis, but is quietly content.

At the top of the hierarchy are "Evangelists" or "Fans." This is the ultimate, the perfect customer who raves about how great you are to everyone they know. The following are some real world examples of your best marketing tool, "Evangelists":

• Apple Customers who line up days before a new product or version comes on the market

• Star Wars or Star Trek fans sitting outside the movie theater 24 hours before the latest film debuts

• Parade goers at the Rose Parade

• Harry Potter fans waiting in line to buy the new book

• Video Game consumers whenever the newest Call of Duty is released

If you want to see what "Sports Evangelists" look like, you can watch them at football games on television. They are the diehard fans sitting in a stadium all bundled up in below-freezing temperatures. These loyal, passionate, and committed fans leave their warm houses to drive on treacherous roads just to watch their favorite team play. These are the kinds of customers you need to cultivate and attract.

## HOW MANY GOOD CUSTOMERS DO YOU HAVE?

When I meet with clients for SCORE counseling, I ask them three questions:

1. How many customers/clients do you have?
2. How many good customers do you have?
3. What are the criteria for a good customer?

I am always amazed by how many small-business owners do not know the answers to these questions. They know how much money they take in. They know how to quantify the money. But they do not know how to count and determine the quality of their customers.

The first step in knowing how to use your best customers to grow your business is to start counting how many customers you have.

When I worked on the Nissan Motors account at Chiat/Day, I would visit dealers around the country where they would spend a lot of time showing me around their beautiful dealerships.

Because I was interested to learn how our retail advertising was doing in terms of driving people into the dealership, I would always ask about their weekend traffic. When I talked to dealers and sales managers, they had an answer that made them sound like they knew what was going on. "Traffic was up. Traffic was down. Traffic was about normal." Whatever the answer, they acted like they had a good handle on the number of people who visited their showroom.

Then, on one of my visits I met with one of the very best automotive dealers in the entire country. This dealer sold more cars and trucks than anyone else in the United States. When I asked him this same question about his traffic, he said, "Hold on a minute, let me go get the report." In a few minutes he came back with a very detailed spreadsheet, which gave the number of people who came into the dealership each day compared to the number who came in one week ago and one year ago.

When I asked him how he compiled this report, he said, "Did you notice that when you came into the parking lot you entered through a gate that went up and down? Well, we first count the number of cars who come into the lot." He continued, "Did you notice that when you came into the main showroom there was a greeter who welcomed you to our dealership? That greeter counts every person who walks into our showroom. As a result, at the end of every day we know how many cars entered our parking lot and how many people came into our dealership."

I was so amazed and impressed by this dealer's attention to details that I told him about my visits to the other dealers and asked how they came up with their numbers. He explained, "In many cases, they work backward from the number of cars they sell. Say they sold 10 cars. From this number, they might assume they had 100 people in the dealership or whatever was their desired ratio of traffic to sales. But it is just a guess. The problem with this system is that they can never really determine how well they are doing at closing the ratio between people who are in the dealership and those who actually bought a car. We, on the other hand, want to know everything."

Applying this same logic to you, the small retail-business owner, try to count how much traffic comes into your store. Then measure the ratio of traffic to sales. If you can increase this ratio, your business will grow even if you can't attract more traffic.

Several years ago, after I retired from the ad agency, my wife and I took a cruise. We traveled around the world in 120 days on Regent Cruise Lines. During that time I got to know and became good friends with their President and CEO, Mark Conroy.

One day, as we discussed marketing, I asked, "How many customers do you have?" Without hesitating, he answered, "We have two thousand customers." I was impressed.

So I asked him the next question, "How many good customers do you have?" And once again without hesitating, he responded, "We have two hundred good customers." I was even more impressed.

But what really blew me away was when I asked, "What are your criteria for a good customer?" He quickly replied, "Two hundred nights on our ships; if someone has sailed with us for two hundred nights they are a very good customer."

Over the next couple of years, Regent developed a loyalty program called The Seven Seas Society, whereby customers would earn more benefits—such as priority boarding and online reservations for shore excursions, etc.—by taking more cruises and spending more nights on Regent's ships.

Regent Cruise Lines' five-tiered loyalty program started with Bronze at the bottom and led up to the Titanium level to designate how many nights their customers had accumulated.

- Titanium – More than 400 nights
- Platinum – 200 to 399 nights
- Gold – 75 to 199 nights
- Silver – 21 to 74 nights
- Bronze – 4 to 20 nights

Actually, when the program first began in 2003, there were only four levels. At that time the top level was Platinum for people with more than 200 nights, as there were only two hundred customers who could fulfill that requirement.

After a few years, however, there were more than one thousand Platinum level customers. The number of good customers had increased by a factor of five times. Overall, the program was so successful that Regent had to create a new top category, Titanium, for people who had spent more than 400 nights on their cruise line.

By providing a ladder of benefits, Regent Cruise Lines created a way to encourage their customers to become even better customers. Whenever my wife and I spent time on a Regent ship, other passengers would take delight in telling us and other customers about all the fantastic Gold, Platinum, or Titanium-level benefits they received. These "Evangelists" were teaching other guests how to become better customers for the cruise line.

Now let's get back to you and your business. After you count your customers (don't guess, really count them), you need some quantifiable way to determine what is your definition of a good customer, such as the number of nights on a ship, how many times someone plays a round of golf, or the total dollars spent, etc. The important thing here is to make it easy for you and for the customer to keep track of where they are in your system. You want them to aspire to reach the next level.

Mark Conroy could have counted any number of things. He could have added up the cruises a person took or how much money was spent, but he decided it was easier for both the cruise line and the customers to count the number of nights they spent on board a Regent ship.

Lastly, once you know who your good customers are, stay in touch with them. Send emails or letters; keep them informed about how they can become even better customers and earn more benefits; offer better service or anything that allows your business to be more valuable to them.

## EXAMPLES OF ATTRACTING MORE GOOD CUSTOMERS

### AMERICAN EXPRESS

*Overhaul Customer Service:*
*"How can we get customers to feel better about us and recommend us to friends?"*
*The result was 10-15% increase in spending & 4-5 times increase in retention.*

### REGENT CRUISE LINES

*Membership Programs*

# HOW TO PROMOTE
# ONE BENEFIT

Price

Quality/
Performance

Service/
Convenience

# Chapter 9

# HOW TO PROMOTE ONE BENEFIT

I first learned about the importance of promoting one benefit when I was a young man in my twenties. I wanted to crew on the big sailboats that raced every week out of the California Yacht Club in Marina Del Rey, California.

The yacht club published a magazine for members in which anyone could buy short little classified ads like you see on a bulletin board. To get the attention of the members who raced in the club, I wrote my first ad: "Crew Available."

For hours, days, weeks, I waited for the phone to ring with any kind of acknowledgement, but none came.

Unwilling to give up, I decided I needed to rethink my approach. Instead of talking about me and my availability, I focused on what the boat owners might want, which was to cross the finish line first. They were looking for crew members who could help them tack their boats in a fast and efficient manner so they could win the race.

So I sat down at my desk and rewrote my ad, choosing one benefit of hiring me to crew on a sailboat: "Fastest Grinder in the West."

The results were amazing. In a few days I had offers to sail on several of the best boats in the yacht club and it was all because I promoted one benefit that was relevant to my target audience.

Before I begin to talk about how to promote one benefit, I want to explain why this is so important in helping you get and retain more great customers.

There is a natural tendency for all of us to believe that more is better. Many of my SCORE clients ask me, "Why should I limit my marketing by focusing on just one benefit when my product or service has several benefits?"

This is a good question, actually. However, I can think of several reasons why you should not try to promote more than one benefit.

The first reason has to do with the reality of our modern world. We live in a complex and complicated society. There are hundreds of thousands of products and services that we as consumers can purchase. Visit your local supermarket and count the number of different brands of cereal or toilet paper or most products on the shelves. There are even variations within the choices of one single product. For example, there are twelve varieties of Cheerios alone: Original Cheerios, Multi-Grain, Honey Nut, Apple Cinnamon, Banana Nut, Frosted, Cinnamon Burst, Multi-Grain Cheerios Peanut Butter, Dulce de Leche, Chocolate, Fruity Cheerios, and Yogurt Burst.

Second, we are bombarded by messages about these products on television, in radio ads, newspapers and magazines, on the Internet and billboards, on our smartphones, and in movie theaters—virtually everywhere we go and in everything we do. As consumers, we are desperately looking for simplicity, not more complexity. In a world of abundance, we seek simple shortcuts to help us cope and organize the world around us.

The main reason that you must find your product or service's one benefit is to keep it simple and consistent so that the consumer can remember you and what you can do for them. Your job as a marketer is to make it easy and simple for consumers who also want to know that:

- Tide gets the dirt out
- Crest prevents cavities
- Walmart has the lowest prices
- BMW is the ultimate driving machine
- Pepsi is the choice of a new generation
- Coca Cola is the real thing
- Maxwell House Coffee is good to the last drop
- Disneyland is the Happiest Place on Earth
- Everything is easier on a Mac

By linking your product to one simple benefit you provide a shortcut for consumers in the same way that we use nicknames for people, like "Honest Abe" and "Stonewall Jackson."

Your job as a smart marketer is to help prospective consumers figure out the critical benefits about your product or service as quickly and as easily as possible. As a consumer, you want to know:

- What does this product/service do?
- Is it for me?
- How and when does it fit into my life?
- How is it different/better than what already exists?
- Why should I believe or trust this product/service?

Another reason not to promote more than one benefit is because you want to be something specific for a very targeted audience. You want to solve isolated problems or needs for a select group of people.

Remember all the emphasis I placed on knowing your target audience? No matter how hard you try to please everyone, you can't. You only want to please your target. So, what specific benefits are most important to your target? Don't forget, you are trying to match who and what you are with someone else's needs and wants.

Think about yourself as a consumer. Most of us can come up with one or two words to describe what benefits we like in our favorite products, services, or brands. I'll use myself as an example. Here are simple one or two-word benefits I associate with some of my favorite brands.

| Brand | Benefit(s) |
|---|---|
| Chipotle | Fast/Easy |
| Amazon.com | Great Selection/Easy to Purchase |
| L.L. Bean | Good Quality/Return Policy |
| Charles Shaw Wine (Two Buck Chuck) | Low Price |
| Apple | Great Aesthetics/Ease of Use |
| Nordstrom | Great Service |

It is easy for us to do this as a consumer, but often difficult as a business owner or marketer. It's hard to pick and choose just one or two benefits because we believe we have so many more. We are confident that our products are great quality, our customer service is flawless, and our prices and selection are outstanding. Like a new parent, we are proud and we want other people to share our pride.

During my 10 years working on the Nissan Motors, USA, account, we tried to help the client choose a single benefit to promote the brand. Based on all the available research back in 1988, the primary distinctive benefit of a Nissan was "Fun to Drive", obviously influenced by the Datsun 240Z Sports Car.

It turned out that the Nissan executives were reluctant to accept this recommendation and ultimately rejected it. They believed that it was too narrow, too limiting, too small an audience. However, that was precisely the point. In *Marketing Without Money* you want to have a limited, defined audience. You want to promote a simple, relevant benefit that will resonate with your target.

## WHAT DO YOU STAND FOR?

It is difficult to promote one benefit if you do not know what your business or brand stands for. Apple stands for ease of use, so it is logical that they promote this benefit. Nike stands for athletic performance; Target stands for low prices with style; Volvo stands for safety, etc.

Now, let's turn the tables. What does your business stand for? What are you trying to do? What is the purpose of your business?

In business, as in life, perspective is very important. One of my favorite stories is about a man who asked three different bricklayers what they were doing. The first one answered, "I am laying bricks." The second said, "I am building a wall." The third bricklayer responded, "I am building a cathedral." Even though these three people all appeared to be doing the exact same thing, they each had a unique perspective about what they were doing.

What is your perspective? Are you just selling stuff or are you honestly trying to solve your clients' needs? Are you trying to make money or are you making the world a better place?

Some people call this a mission statement or a vision. No matter what it's labeled, it comes down to understanding your agenda, your purpose, your "why!"

As I mentioned earlier, Simon Sinek does a great job of explaining the importance of knowing why we are in business in his book, *Start With Why: How Great Leaders Inspire Everyone To Take Action*. Sinek also gives us great examples of successful companies that have incorporated their "why" into every facet of their marketing program.

Finally, you should promote one benefit because this is how our brains work. As consumers, our minds function like sorting boxes or filing cards. We have categories in our brain for all kinds of things. There's one for retail stores so that when we encounter names like Walmart or Nordstrom, we're able to put these stores in the right place within our filing system.

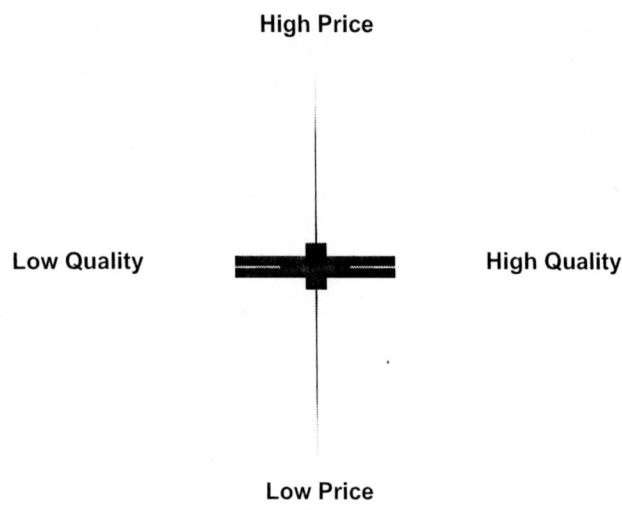

In marketing, this is called "Positioning," which is just a fancy word for categorizing things in our brain. Positioning is about placing products or brands in geographic relationship to one another. The graphic above, for example, is a simple positioning map with just two dimensions: quality and price. Now, let's impose some brands on the following positioning map. Given these two dimensions, here's where I would position Nordstrom versus Walmart.

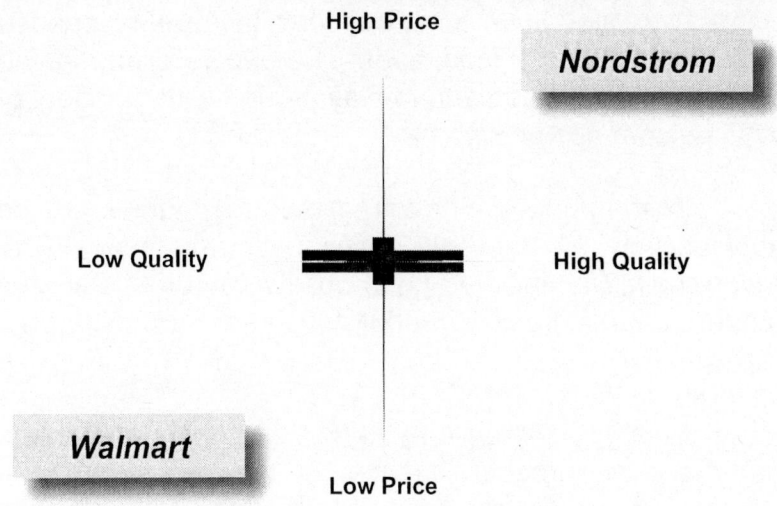

Where, in your opinion, would you place other stores? Where would you place Target, JC Penney or Macy's? The following is another positioning map with again, two dimensions, but switching out price for service.

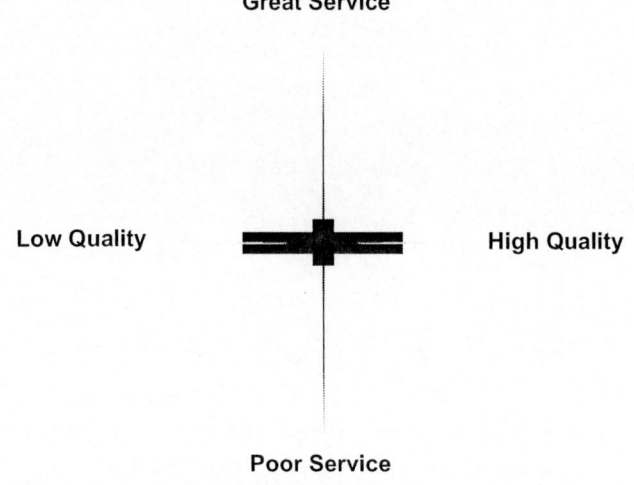

Now do this exercise again. Would you change the position of Nordstrom or Walmart? Where would you put Target on this map? How about JC Penney and Macy's?

Once you have done this for retail brands, choose a different category. How about sports cars or the airline industry? I encourage you to play around with a variety of positioning maps until you feel comfortable.

The important thing to remember is that there is no right answer. We are only dealing with your perception. If you think Walmart has good quality, then that's all that matters. Marketing is all about consumer perception, not reality.

Finally, you should try to do a few positioning maps for your own product, service, or brand. For starters, you can use the elementary benefit segmentation I have referred to on Page 117 and below. Do you want to promote low prices, your quality products, or outstanding customer service?

I have repeatedly emphasized that this benefit segmentation is only the most basic. Within each of these three segments there are several more sub-segments. For example, Quality/Performance can be further segmented into the following more-specific benefits:

- Reliability
- Durability

- Speed
- Resale Value
- Reputation, etc.

Consequently, instead of promoting "quality," which is kind of a vague benefit, you could promote something more specific about your quality. For example, you could promote a lifetime warranty or guaranteed satisfaction. You might even decide to promote a single component of your benefit like Wendy's Restaurant did when it featured its hamburgers as "Hot & Juicy."

Likewise, Service/Convenience can be even further segmented as:

- Close Proximity
- Friendly/Helpful
- Fast, etc.

Instead of promoting "great service," you could highlight a specific component like Federal Express did with their slogan, "Absolutely Positively by 10:00 a.m." Another great example is the one clear benefit of the U.S. Post Office that I mentioned earlier, "If it Fits, it Ships."

Using this information as a background, it's time for you to go to work. Answer the following questions about your business, your product or service, or your brand:

1.  What does your business stand for? What are your core principles? What is your purpose, your perspective? Why are you in business?

Remember, the way you run your business should reflect and be in harmony with these principles. If you want to serve customer needs, you have to ask them what they want and how you can do a better job of satisfying those needs. If you want to stand for great customer service, you need to be willing to hire enough competent people to deliver this service. If you stand for honesty, you don't tell lies or half-truths. If you stand for cleanliness, you don't have dirty restrooms.

As my former boss, Jay Chiat, used to say, "It isn't a core principle until it costs you money." At Chiat/Day we did not solicit clients who sold cigarettes, even though in the 1970s there was a lot of money to be made advertising such a product. It was a "core principle." Refusing to do this cost the agency money. That's what Jay Chiat meant when he made the statement.

Now you are ready for the big question.

2.   What do you want to be known for?

The answer to this question should be the one benefit you want to promote. If you want to be known for great quality, do not promote low prices. If you want to be known for great service, satisfy your customers' needs and wants.

As a small, relatively new business, you have a lot of flexibility. Since few people know of your existence, you do not need to worry about past perceptions. You can start to shape your customers' opinions by how you act and what you promote. You just need to be consistent. Most people associate Volvo with safety because they have steadily promoted this one benefit for more than 20 years.

As a SCORE Counselor, I could promote myself in a number of ways. I could highlight my experience working with big clients and big budgets or my 10 years of helping small-business owners with free counseling, developing marketing plans, etc. Instead, I chose to focus on one benefit—Marketing Without Money—because I know that this is the benefit with which most small-business owners can relate.

Once you've had a chance to digest the information in this chapter, you need to decide, "What is the primary benefit you want to promote?"

## EXAMPLES OF PROMOTING ONE BENEFIT

### WALMART

*Low Prices*

### CHIAT/DAY

*Breakthrough Creativity*

### VOLVO

*Safety*

### FEDERAL EXPRESS

*Absolutely Positively by 10:00 a.m.*

### WENDY'S

*Hot & Juicy*

### TOM PATTY (CREW)

*Fastest Grinder in the West*

### TOM PATTY (SCORE)

*Marketing Without Money*

# HOW TO IMPROVE YOUR VALUE EQUATION

$$value = \frac{benefits}{cost}$$

# Chapter 10

# HOW TO IMPROVE
# YOUR VALUE EQUATION

On a scale of 1-10 (10 being the best), rate the value equation for your product or service. Now, think about how you can improve this rating.

Most people put too much importance on price. Instead, I want you to focus on value. Price, in the end, means little. If price was everything, nobody would pay $250,000 for an automobile. You can get a car that does many of the things a $250,000 car does for much less. So, the value of a product is what's important. If something has no value to somebody, getting "two for the price of one" is not a benefit.

When determining the value of something, we must ask ourselves, "How important is the expense relative to the perceived value of benefits I will get from it?"

Let's look at some simple examples. You go to the airport with a bottle of water that costs you less than a dollar. But you cannot take it through the Airport TSA Security Checkpoint. So you throw the bottle away. Now, if you want to buy another bottle of water inside the terminal it will cost you more than two or three dollars. Would you be willing to pay twice or triple the amount for the same item? If you want the benefit of quenching your thirst, you must shell out for the inflated price.

Remember, the value of something is entirely personal. What's valuable to one person may not be perceived as a value to another. It's more than a number. It depends on how much you care about getting the benefit at that moment. How important is safety? How important is clean? How important is healthy? How important is that bottle of water inside the airport terminal?

The cost of a first-class airline ticket may be several times greater than the price of coach. It doesn't matter whether you pay $200 or $2,000; the airplane still gets you to the same place at the same time.

This example is an interesting argument. First class does offer a lot of amenities compared to business or coach, but are you willing to pay for a larger seat, the right to board earlier, and a better meal? The answers depend upon what you value.

Whatever we purchase, whether it's an airline ticket, a meal at McDonald's, a new car, or a massage, our brains run through the calculation, "Value = Benefits Divided by Cost."

Before purchasing a product or service, we always ask ourselves, "Do I think this is worth it? What benefits will I get from it? How important are these benefits to me at this exact moment?"

If you are in a hurry or late for a meeting, you may value speed over quality. If you are celebrating a special occasion, more importance may be placed on ordering an expensive bottle of wine.

To improve the value equation of your product or service, you must either increase the benefits or reduce the price.

JC Penney is a great case study in a business that tried to improve its value by constantly cutting its prices. After years of this strategy, they realized that only 2% of all sales were made at full price, with some of those sales purchased at a 50% discount or more. They were spending $1.2 billion on promotion just to attract people into their stores and then selling their merchandise at little or no profit.

This strategy didn't work for JC Penney. It didn't work for GM or Chrysler, and it won't work for you. I'll say it again, "If you cannot buy things as cheaply as Walmart, you cannot compete with them on price." A much better strategy to improve your value equation is to increase your benefits.

It all comes down to really understanding your customers and what they value. You can increase the value just by understanding how you can provide a better experience or product for your customer.

# EXAMPLES OF IMPROVING VALUE EQUATION

## APPLE

*New Features/Same Price*

## CHIAT/DAY

*Added "Account Planning" Service*

## PIZZA HUT

*Created Delivery Service*

## SCORE

*Added More Seminars*

## REGENT CRUISE LINES

*Free Internet & Laundry Service
for Platinum Level Guests*

# HOW TO UNDERSTAND AND USE THE PURCHASE FUNNEL

## Chapter 11

# HOW TO UNDERSTAND AND USE THE PURCHASE FUNNEL

### WHAT IS THE PURCHASE FUNNEL?

I was first introduced to the concept of the Purchase Process in 1978 by Dennis Stefani when he was the Marketing Director for our client, Yamaha Motorcycles, USA. (Dennis is better known as the father of Gwen Stefani of No Doubt fame.)

The idea of the Purchase Process or the Purchase Funnel is that in making a decision about what products or services to buy, all consumers move through several different phases or stages, beginning with AWARENESS, ending with the PURCHASE, and subsequently, the consumer's degree of satisfaction with their purchase, hopefully LOVE.

I like to think of this process as an opportunity for the marketer to lead the prospective consumer on a journey. For the customer, the journey may begin in ignorance. They might not even know of the product's existence, which is frequently the case with many of my small-business clients. So the first job of the marketer is to say, "I exist. Pay attention to me."

This journey continues as the marketer attempts to provide more information including both rational and emotional reasons to support the consumer's ultimate purchase of this product or service.

## Purchase Funnel

Awareness
Consider
Shop
Intend
Buy
Love

As you can see above, the Purchase Funnel is much wider at the top and very narrow at the bottom. Its shape emphasizes the fact that many people do not get all the way to the bottom, or as marketing people like to call it, slippage. The job of the marketer is to get as many potential customers as possible from the top to the bottom of the funnel.

Let's start with a simple example. Say that there is a new movie just out and I want to convince my wife, Susan, to come along. The conversation might go something like this:

"Hey Susan, did you know there is a new James Bond film out called *Skyfall*? Do you want to go see it with me?"

## AWARENESS

The first stage of six in the Purchase Funnel is called AWARENESS. We have to be aware that something exists–a new product, service, or in this case, a movie. Let's assume Susan is aware of the new James Bond film already because she has seen the preview on TV.

"Yes, I've heard about it." Susan says, then asks me a few questions: "What do the reviews say? Do you know anyone who has seen it? What did they think?"

## CONSIDERATION

Generally, one of the best ways to move the consumer from AWARENESS to the CONSIDERATION phase is to provide new, relevant and compelling information.

"Yes, as a matter of fact," I reply. "My brother, John, saw it and said it was really cool. There's a 30-minute car chase and a 15-minute helicopter chase, and the new James Bond, Daniel Craig, is really great."

Even though Susan has been provided with more information, she is still not convinced and asks, "Well that sounds interesting, but there's also a new movie out called *Anna Karenina* that I would like to see."

This brings us to the SHOPPING phase, where the potential customer, in this case, Susan, considers what other options are available.

## SHOPPING

In the SHOPPING phase, Susan asks, "What else is playing at the theatre?" Shopping always involves comparisons between different options, which means that I really need to go to work. I have to quickly think of a good reason why Susan would want to go see the James Bond film, rather than the chick-flick, *Anna Karenina*.

Again, I need to figure out how to move Susan from the SHOPPING phase to the INTENTION phase, where she could possibly concede.

Let's say, to sweeten the deal I come up with a reciprocity strategy by offering, "If you go to the Bond movie with me today, next Tuesday I will take you to see *Anna Karenina* then dinner afterwards."

## INTENTION

With Susan accepting my offer, we have now moved to the INTENTION phase, which equates to both of us intending to get in the car and drive to the theatre to see the Bond film. We are still a long way from actually buying the tickets, however.

I'm sure that most of us have intended to do things that we didn't actually do. We intended to go to the gym on Tuesday, but we didn't. We put something in a shopping cart, but never actually purchased it. Intention just means that we plan to do something.

## BUY

Just to keep the story moving forward, let's say that Susan and I actually got to the theatre, purchased the tickets, and in the end, saw the movie. So the game is now over, right? Not really. You might remember me saying that good marketers do not think that someone buying their product or service is the goal. Steve Jobs didn't want you to just buy an iPad. He ultimately wanted you to LOVE it.

## LOVE

My story continues; unfortunately, for me, it does not have a happy ending. When the film ends and Susan and I come out of the movie theater, she does not LOVE it. She wasn't impressed with *Skyfall's* 30-minute car chase or the 15-minute helicopter chase. She wasn't even that taken with Daniel Craig as 007. As a result, I can't really see Susan going to another Bond film with me in the near future.

Remember, the goal of marketing is not just to "sell stuff" but rather to create a positive experience with a product or service so they will want to repeat it. It's not just about getting more customers. You want more "Evangelists" who tell others how great you are.

The Purchase Funnel is generally the process we go through whether we are buying a car, purchasing an item of clothing, deciding to get married, or going to the movies. It is not necessarily rational. Many times, we use our rational brain to justify our emotions.

## PURCHASE FUNNEL EXAMPLE: APPLE iPHONE

In my seminars, I demonstrate the reality of the Purchase Funnel by using the example of the Apple iPhone, literally one of the most successful products in the history of the world.

First, I get everyone in the class to stand up. Then I announce, "If you've never heard of the Apple iPhone, sit down." Obviously, everyone on the planet is AWARE of the Apple iPhone, so the entire audience remains standing. The iPhone has 100% awareness.

Then we go down the Purchase Funnel. I propose, "If you have never CONSIDERED buying an Apple iPhone, sit down." At this point two or three people follow my request.

My next instruction is, "If you have never SHOPPED for an Apple iPhone, sit down," and a few more people take their seats.

Then comes, "If you have never INTENDED to buy an Apple iPhone, sit down," and again a small number does so.

Finally I say, "If you have never BOUGHT an Apple iPhone, sit down." At this point, if there are 100 people in the room there are now about 10 or 12 attendees left standing.

At last we come to the most important part of the Purchase Funnel. I now know that everyone still standing owns an Apple iPhone, so I add, "If you do not LOVE your iPhone, sit down."

To date, I have conducted this demonstration more than a hundred times with literally thousands of people in my seminars, and generally, every single time almost everyone remains standing. Sometimes, rarely, one, two, maybe three people take their seats, but more often than not I am amazed that virtually everyone loves their Apple products.

The purpose of this exercise is to demonstrate two things. The first is to show how difficult it is to move people down the Purchase Funnel. In this case, we start with 100 people for one of the most popular products on the planet and we end up with maybe 10% to 15% who have actually purchased it.

The second point this exercise reminds us of is that it's about diminution. In other words, we start with a lot of people and slowly they fall out of the process or the Purchase Funnel.

In Apple's instance we start with 100% awareness. With most of my small-business clients, however, the awareness of their product, even among their target audience, is almost never 100%. If one of the most popular products in the world loses 85% to 90% of the people as they move through the Purchase Funnel, what percentage will the average small business lose?

I'm not going to lie to you, creating AWARENESS for your product can be very expensive. Whenever we launched a new Nissan product at the agency we generally had an advertising budget of about $100,000,000. Spending this kind of money on television and other broadcast media could guarantee a certain level of awareness within a relatively short period of time. But of course, not one of my small-business clients has a $100,000,000 or even a $1,000 advertising budget.

Many people believe that they can solve this awareness gap by using social media or search-engine optimization. However, the reality is that for every YouTube video that goes viral and gets 100,000 views, there are millions that few people see.

In order to create awareness efficiently, you need to be reminded of your clearly defined target. Not everyone NEEDS to be aware of your product or service, only those customers or clients who are likely to make a purchase.

Now, try to imagine how your product or service would do in this previous demonstration. How many people would have to sit down because they are not aware of your product or service? How many potential customers would you lose at each phase in this process?

Another good mental exercise is to think about the last purchase you made, whether it was a pair of shoes, a car, or even a stick of gum. The time it takes to move through the purchase process can vary from a few seconds for a stick of gum to six months for a new car. But really think about what moved you through this process. What was important to you in each of these phases or stages?

To help you move your Internet customers down the Purchase Funnel, I have designed the following step-by-step chart, but of course it works the same for real-world retailers.

| HOW TO MOVE YOUR CUSTOMERS DOWN THE PURCHASE FUNNEL (Acronym: GO GET ROI LOVE) | |
|---|---|
| **GO** | **GO** where they are (Awareness) |
| **G** | **GET** their attention (Awareness) |
| **E** | **ENGAGE** them by letting them sample or play for free. (Demonstrate/Consider) |
| **T** | **TRADE** something for email (Reciprocity/ Consider) |
| **R** | **ROUTE** them to landing page (Consider) |
| **O** | Create **OFFER** designed to get prospect to put something in shopping cart (Intention) |
| **I** | Provide extra **INCENTIVE** to close deal NOW (Buy) |
| **LOVE** | Make it easy for the customer to let others know how much they **LOVE** your products or services. (LOVE) |

## GO WHERE THEY ARE (AWARENESS)

The first step is to generate awareness among your target audience. Please repeat this aloud: "You do not need everyone in the world to be aware of your product or service, only the people who are most likely to buy."

Go where they are. Go where your target audience goes. If your best prospects are at track meets, go to track meets. If they are at trade shows, go to trade shows. You also need to know where your target audience goes on the Internet. What websites do they use? What blogs do they read? The example I use in my seminars is the website, AcousticGuitar.com. If you want to reach people who play acoustic guitar, this is a good place to find them.

## GET THEIR ATTENTION (AWARENESS)

Once you know where to find your target audience, you need to attract their attention. If you are going to a trade show, you'll need to create a display booth that will entice people over to ask questions. If you are trying to reach acoustic guitar players who want to improve at playing the guitar, you can advertise on the Lesson Page of AcousticGuitar.com.

It's not enough just to run an ad with Google AdSense anymore. You have to be clever. You have to be creative. Remember, you are competing for someone's attention. A clever headline will generate thousands of responses compared to something boring and dull.

Which of the two following headlines do you feel is more interesting and effective?

**GET BETTER AT THE GUITAR**

or

**LEARN TO PLAY A BLUES SONG
WITH ONLY 3 NOTES**

Clearly, the second example is more compelling. It provides a simple benefit. It sounds easy enough that the reader thinks, "I can do that."

## ENGAGE YOUR PROSPECTS (DEMONSTRATE/ CONSIDER)

The best example of a business that does a great job of engaging their customers is, you guessed it, the Apple Store. The entire layout is designed specifically to get you engaged in their products. When you walk into an Apple Store you are surrounded by a room full of tables that are the perfect height to stand next to (sitting is sometimes too much of a commitment), where you are encouraged to play with the merchandise. Apple wants you to touch and use with their products. Unlike many retail stores where products are protected in plastic encasements or boxes, the iPads, iPhones, MacBooks, etc. are right there for you to touch and feel to the point of falling in love. This is the ultimate way to engage your prospective clients.

If you own a retail business you need to understand that your store must be better—more engaging, informative, and interesting than your website. If it isn't, there is absolutely no reason for it to exist.

I am always amazed when I go into a retail store and find that they are actually less customer-friendly than their website. Thanks to Apple, the bar has been raised. To be a successful retailer in today's marketplace you have to provide something you can't get on the Internet. Maybe it's the ability to try on a sweater or the salesperson actually knows something about the product that you can't learn from a website. Again, Apple is a perfect example. Their sales technicians can answer any questions you could possibly have. They even provide classes and forums for learning, way beyond what you can get online.

At this stage, when people are in your store, you are trying to move them down the Purchase Funnel, so you need to take them from Awareness to Consideration. Generally, the best way to achieve this is to demonstrate how the product or service will help the consumer in some way. Will it solve a problem? What are the most compelling benefits of the product or service? If you are trying to get someone to CONSIDER an iPhone, you show them the cool apps that are available and all of the other benefits an iPhone will give them.

## TRADE SOMETHING (RECIPROCITY/CONSIDER)

This technique is especially effective in Internet marketing. The idea here is to offer the prospect something of value for free. My SCORE colleague, Jerome Chiaro, who teaches courses on Internet Marketing, advocates, "Give away your best stuff for free." Let's say you give away a short one-minute video guitar tip or lesson. Then you offer the prospect another free lesson if they give you their email address. This concept only works if you actually provide something the prospect values.

Examples of reciprocity marketing are all around us. Before you purchase a book on iBooks on the iPad, you can sample it for free, no strings attached. This is amazing. If you are a fast reader you might be able to read the whole book without ever buying it. But they trust you not to take advantage of the concept.

Again, as Jerome correctly points out, "The biggest hurdle to overcome on the Internet is TRUST. No one knows who they can trust or who is going to take their credit card and go to Burma."

The best Internet Marketers engage in Relationship Marketing where it is more about establishing a trusting connection with customers than it is about making a sale. Zappos encourages people to order shoes in different sizes to make sure they get what they want. Then they make it easy and free to send back their discards. Again, this is a great example of a business trusting customers not to abuse the concept.

In today's marketplace, consumers look for businesses that they can trust to deliver satisfaction. A good way to build trust is to show that you trust them. Instead of assuming everyone will take advantage of your kindness, good marketers believe that most people will treat them fairly and not abuse their trust.

Another example of Relationship Marketing is L.L. Bean. If, for any reason you are not satisfied, you can send the merchandise back and get a refund. They even pay for your return postage.

## ROUTE PROSPECT TO LANDING PAGE (CONSIDER)

We are now at the level in the Purchase Funnel where you try to get your prospect to strongly CONSIDER buying your product or service.

It's at this point where the consumer will start to think about what other competitive options are available. Where else can I buy this for less money? Is this iPhone worth the extra cost versus the less expensive alternatives? This is where you seize the opportunity to convince the prospect that this is not only a good product or service, but that it's better than the other products on the market. In marketing, this is called the Competitive Advantage. Not all products or services have an easily identifiable Competitive Advantage. But a good marketer will usually be able to either find one or create one.

With the wide usage of smartphones, this phase has become even more competitive. Many shoppers will use their cell phone to compare prices.

Southwest Airlines has a terrific Competitive Advantage. Unlike most of their competition, they do not charge you to check your luggage.

Hyundai has created an interesting Competitive Advantage as well, guaranteeing a certain buy-back price on every new car they sell. This provides the customer with a sense of what this car will be worth when they are ready to trade it in, another example of building trust in the relationship.

## CREATE AN OFFER (INTENTION)

Once the prospect has moved beyond the CONSIDERATION and SHOPPING phases, they reach the INTENTION phase. This is the stage in the Purchase Funnel where you try to get the prospect to actually do something. You want them to signal that they INTEND to buy. On the Internet or in a retail store, this is accomplished when someone puts something in their shopping cart.

The prospect still hasn't purchased anything yet, but he or she has indicated by their behavior that they INTEND to purchase. Keep in mind, however, intention is a tricky thing. I use the example of the people who have signed up, paid for, and registered for my Marketing Without Money seminars, but did not actually show up. These are called no-shows. On the Internet there is a substantially higher rate of abandonment. In other words, people put things in the shopping cart, but do not end up actually purchasing them.

There can be thousands of reasons for this. Maybe the person was distracted by a phone call or an interruption of some sort. They could have second thoughts about the purchase and want more time to think about it. Worse yet, maybe there's a glitch in your website that makes it difficult for the potential customer to follow through with their purchase. This happens all the time.

Infomercials provide some terrific examples of how you can attempt to move someone down the Purchase Funnel from CONSIDERATION to INTENTION. Generally, it's by offering incentive for an action such as, "This price is only good for the next 24 hours," or "We only have two more of this item in stock." You need to create some incentive to overcome the inertia of not acting now.

A SCORE client of mine who sells beautiful photographs of exotic cars recently had an online sale where he reduced the price of his artwork. By highlighting the very limited availability of the selected items, he sold more than 20 photographs in two days, many times more than his usual volume.

In my opinion, at this stage in the Purchase Funnel, you do not want to introduce other options. In fact, you want to eliminate additional choices. If you are shopping at Tiffany's, looking at jewelry, this is the point where the good salesperson removes the other alternatives and gets you to focus on the benefits and beauty of one selected item. You do not want any distractions.

## PROVIDE EXTRA INCENTIVE TO CLOSE DEAL NOW (BUY)

Once someone has put your product in their shopping cart, you want to get them to push the "Buy Now" button as quickly as possible. This applies to both Internet and retail shopping. Many times I have picked out things that I wanted to buy in a store. But when I went to pay for the items, there was a long line at the check-out counter. I've said to myself, "It's not worth the wait," abandoned my shopping cart behind a clothing rack, and departed.

This is why you want the distance between INTENTION and BUY to be as short and as quick as possible. The customer has come a long way down the Purchase Funnel. He or she is literally at your doorstep, so answer the door and let them in.

One of the most creative ideas I have seen on the Internet was an actual timer that started counting down the minutes the instant you put something in the shopping cart until you hit the "Buy Now" button. If you completed the transaction in 30 seconds or less, you received an extra bonus—free overnight shipping or an additional discount.

Another way to close the deal is the use of Coupon Codes. According to Jerome, "The feeling people get is amazing when they enter their code in the box at checkout and see the price drop in half."

## MAKE IT EASY TO SPREAD THE LOVE (Love)

The final destination on the journey through the Purchase Funnel is LOVE. The true goal of a good marketer isn't just to "sell stuff"; the goal is to create customers who LOVE you and tell their friends about your great products or services. So how do you do this? You do it by making it easy for customers to spread positive word-of-mouth.

In terms of spreading the love, "The best way to get testimonials is to ask," says Jerome. I have also found this to be true. If you know who your best customers are (and you should), simply ask them to give you a testimonial. You will be surprised how easy it is.

A great way to spread the word on the Internet is to provide a "Share with a Friend" link that facilitates easy spreading. All good marketers understand the importance of communicating with your customers after the sale. However, many Internet marketers do not take advantage of the opportunity to follow up. You already have their email. You know how to reach them. Ask them to give you feedback on their experience or mention other products or services they may be interested in. As Jerome says, "If you don't follow up, you are leaving a lot of money on the table."

I know at first the Purchase Funnel may sound complicated. But like everything in marketing, it is what we do every day in our own lives.

So, what exactly are you doing in the Purchase Funnel to move your customers down to the next phase? I can tell you one thing—if you follow my advice you will definitely attract new customers, increase your sales, and grow your business.

# HOW TO USE THE RIGHT STRATEGY TO GROW YOUR BUSINESS

## Growth Strategies

%          %

**More $ from existing customers**          **More new customers**

## Chapter 12

# HOW TO USE THE RIGHT STRATEGY TO GROW YOUR BUSINESS

You may have wondered, "What are the different ways I can grow my business?" From the largest perspective, there are really only two ways to increase your business and revenues:

1.  Get more money from your existing customers, or
2.  Get more new customers

(Note: There is actually a third way, which is to merge or acquire, but it does not apply to small businesses that need to grow before they can consider this strategy.)

## GROWTH STRATEGY #1: Get More Money From Existing Customers

The reason that I like this strategy is because it is by far the most efficient way to grow your business. In other words, it costs the least. This is a core strategy for the concept of *Marketing without Money*.

## SERVICE-ORIENTED BUSINESSES

During the 10 years I managed the Nissan Motors, USA, account at Chiat/Day, we were able to quadruple the agency's revenue by getting more money from this one client. During a 10-year period we increased our revenues from $15 million to more than $60 million. This is called Organic or Internal Growth because, like the growth of a tree, it comes from within.

How did we do this? Initially, we just had one piece of the Nissan advertising budget. However, in 1987, in a competitive shoot-out against three other agencies, we managed to win the Nissan National Advertising account, which was about $150 million in billings, the largest account shift in the history of advertising at that time. The agency received revenues of about 10%, or $15 million a year from this piece of business.

One year later, Nissan consolidated its entire regional advertising budget and gave us another $100 million account called Regional Marketing, which added $10 million a year to our agency revenues.

A short time passed when, without notice, Nissan fired the ad agency that handled the Infiniti account (Nissan's upscale brand) and gave this $100 million account again to our ad agency. This resulted in another $10 million a year for Chiat/Day.

In addition to adding the Regional and Infiniti accounts, we were also able to get Nissan to give us other projects such as Direct Marketing, which added even more earnings to the agency.

In 1996 Chiat/Day was purchased by Omnicom (one of the largest ad agency networks in the world) and merged with another agency called TBWA, which handled the Nissan advertising in Europe, as well as in many other countries around the world. Now, our new agency, TBWA Chiat/Day, controlled the advertising for Nissan in 58 countries. Obviously, this contributed more millions to our revenues.

So, what's the secret to getting more business from your existing clients? The answer is very simple. You have to exceed the client's expectations. The main reason we got the Infiniti account was because we did a fantastic job of launching the Altima for the Nissan Brand. We produced a campaign based on positioning the Altima as the "affordable luxury car" and compared it to the Lexus brand, rather than the obvious competitors, the Toyota Camry or the Honda Accord. The dealers loved this campaign and the Altima launch was one of the most successful in Nissan's history.

Another example of 'Getting More Money from Existing Customers' is my SCORE client, Tasha Oldham, who spent 15 years as a successful documentary filmmaker. Her first film, *The Smith Family*,  was nominated for an Emmy and won the Director's Guild Award, the highest achievement for any director. Tasha has also done work for Disney, Sony Pictures, The Travel Channel, and ABC Television.

But it wasn't enough. She wanted not only to create films; she wanted to own her own company where her vision and standards of excellence could be realized. So, in 2010 she started "My Story, Inc." with no employees, no clients, and no money.

Based on her portfolio and her dynamic personality she was able to hire a staff and attract a few clients, and within the first year she got her first big opportunity. Tasha was hired by SCORE National in Washington D.C. to create a three-minute video that would show how SCORE counselors helped small-business owners.

Tasha did a fabulous job, exceeding everyone's expectations. SCORE loved the finished video and sure enough, she got another much bigger project from SCORE creating 14 television public-service announcements.

Once again Tasha wowed the client, demonstrating not only that she was a great filmmaker, but that she was also a very professional business person who could be counted on to deliver a fantastic product on time and within budget.

Today, Tasha is the founder and CEO of a major film production company with clients ranging from start-up entrepreneurs to mid-size companies, including First Team Real Estate, Deluxe Corporation, and national non--profit organizations like SCORE.

To get more service-oriented business from your existing customers, like Tasha did, make a list of all of your clients. Rank them first by the amount of annual revenue you receive from each one, then base it on the potential they represent for more money. In other words, if one of your clients has a marketing budget of $10 million and you are only getting $1 million, you potentially have a great opportunity to get $9 million more of that budget.

I do need to stress the point, however, that your clients are not just going to hand over more of their budget. You have to earn it. You really have to produce value for your clients; do more and perform better than the other suppliers or vendors. This is a case where "good enough is definitely not enough."

The beauty of this strategy is that you do not need to spend a lot of marketing dollars to implement it. In my example of the Nissan case, sure, the agency spent a ton of money to get the initial business (more than $1 million).

But almost no incremental dollars were used to increase the revenues by adding the Regional, Infiniti, and Direct Marketing pieces.

## PRODUCT-ORIENTED BUSINESSES

If you sell products, there are a number of ways you can get more money from your existing customers. First encourage them to buy your product more frequently. If a customer is purchasing your product once a week, get them to buy it twice a week. If someone is buying a quart of your product, figure out a way to make them buy a half gallon. Create reasons for your customers to buy more quantity and more frequently.

## BUY MORE FREQUENTLY

We have all seen the Mattress Guy on television for Sit 'N Sleep, telling us about the tons of bed bugs we accumulate in our mattress. This campaign is obviously designed to convince us that we need a new mattress every several years.

In another example, a large percentage of the population keeps an open box of Arm & Hammer Baking Soda in their refrigerators to eliminate odors. A number of years ago, Arm & Hammer created a marketing campaign telling us that we should replace the box every three months.

Along those same lines, some toothbrush manufacturers now put color coding on the bristles to indicate when it's time to buy another toothbrush. Computer and software manufacturers are always updating operating systems, which forces us either to upgrade or buy a new computer. Many of the products we buy such as milk, orange juice, and cartons of eggs have an expiration date right on the packaging. In addition to keeping us safe, these are friendly reminders for us to buy more often.

Now it's time to put your thinking caps on. If you are selling a product, surely you can come up with ways to get your customers to buy more frequently.

Another strategy is to increase the size of the average transaction. Look at the value pack at every fast food outlet. Encouraging you to spend more money than just buying the hamburger by itself, the value pack increases the average transaction price.

One of the most obvious examples of this strategy is used in the restaurant industry. When you finish with your entree, your server will try to tempt you with a delicious dessert, and of course everyone knows that the fastest way to increase the size of the check in a restaurant is to sell you another alcoholic beverage. Not only does the amount of the transaction grow, it also has a very high profit margin.

High profit margins in alcohol are grossly evident in Las Vegas nightclubs. Grey Goose Vodka that wholesales for $31 is sold to customers for $545 a bottle. Request a VIP booth down on the dance floor at one of these clubs and you're into a $3,000 to $5,000 tab.

## HOW TO PUT THIS STRATEGY TO WORK FOR YOU

One of the most effective ways to get more money from your existing customers is to communicate with them frequently through email. If you are already a SCORE client, look at how many emails you get every month telling you about another upcoming workshop or seminar. My inbox is also filled with emails from retailers I have purchased from, including L.L. Bean, Orvis, Timberland, etc. They are all using this same strategy: "Get more money from existing customers."

If you are in the retail business, come up with ways to trade something (reciprocity) in exchange for someone giving you their email address. Maybe you could offer them a 10% discount on their purchase or a free gift. It really doesn't matter. What's important is that you are extending a gesture that indicates you want to have a mutually beneficial relationship with your customers.

My most recent experience with reciprocity was at the golf course that I frequent. In exchange for giving my email address to the club and signing up for a tee-time before 8:00 a.m., I was offered the Early Bird Special discount.

It's amazing to me how many small-business owners do not have a database and don't collect email addresses from their clients. Email is one of the most efficient and effective forms of marketing. No matter what business you are in, you need to make it a priority to collect email addresses from all of your customers.

## GROWTH STRATEGY #2: Get More New Customers

The lifeblood of every business is getting new customers. No matter how well you treat your customers or how good a job you do, you will inevitably lose some of them. Jay Chiat used to say that the day we won a new piece of business was the beginning of a time clock that counted down the days or months or years until we lost that client. This is why you always need to be attracting new business.

I've already gone over how to get more new customers for product-based businesses extensively in

Chapter 6, Marketing Leverage. So I'd like to concentrate on this strategy for those of you solely in service-oriented businesses.

## SERVICE-ORIENTED BUSINESSES

The single most efficient way to acquire more new clients in a service-oriented business is to get your satisfied customers to recommend you to others.

When I was at the ad agency, we always tried to use this strategy. If the CEO/Marketing Director of one of our clients was really pleased with our work, we could be pretty sure that they would tell other CEOs/Marketing Directors about us.

In this regard, one of the things every business needs to do is to always be reminding your clients what you have done for them. This should not be done in a self-serving way, but rather in a way that gives your client the credit for the success. The motto here is "Merchandise Your Success." Help your clients get publicity for that great idea you gave them. At Chiat/Day we won a lot of advertising awards and we used those award shows as a way to give thanks and credit to our clients.

If you think about it, you can probably come up with ways to remind your clients of the value you have brought to their business. Everyone likes to be part of something that is successful. Help your client shine and they could become part of your marketing force for new business.

Another key element in winning new business is to understand and get very good at the various steps involved in the new business process. In the advertising industry there are basically four stages in the process of winning new business.

First of all, almost every client with an advertising/ marketing budget of $25 million or more probably already has an advertising agency. So, be aware of what is going on with other clients and their relationships with their agencies. Is the client happy with the agency or disappointed?

In 1983, the Nike advertising account was put "in review" because the executives were not happy with their current agency and they wanted to teach them a lesson. Nike held a review process and hired Chiat/Day, where we had the account for about two years. We did some fantastic work for Nike, including the campaign for the 1984 Olympics in Los Angeles and the introduction of the Air Jordan shoe. Then Nike fired us in 1985 and gave the account back to the previous agency, figuring they had learned their lesson.

In the ad agency industry, the first step in getting most new business is that the client puts its agency "in review." This is a visible and public statement that the agency wants to look at other options. Sometimes the incumbent agency is allowed to participate in the review and other times they are simply fired.

In any case, the first job of winning new business is to get invited to participate in the review, which usually involves filling out a lengthy questionnaire. In other categories of business this process can be called a Request for Proposal (RFP).

Once the agency has been notified that it will be included in the review, a process of elimination begins. Similar to any elimination process, you want to be the one left standing.

The second stage in the process is where the client whittles down the possible contenders to a short list of perhaps five to seven agencies for a Credentials Presentation. How many employees do you have? How many offices? What other clients? At this stage, the agency will be asked to present case studies to show how you have handled other businesses that may be relevant to this client and category.

In the Pitch Stage, the client shortens the list even more to the final three to five agencies that get to present elaborate pitches to the client. These remaining few agencies spend several months and millions of dollars and hours researching, creating strategies for campaign ideas and commercials, and putting together their final pitch in which they will try to demonstrate why the client should hire them over the other contenders. We can reduce all of this to the following stages:

- The Long List (Invitation to Participate)
- The Short List (Credentials Presentation)
- The Final List (The Pitch)
- The Winner

Many service businesses go through some variation of this process, and in order to be successful in your new business you must be great at every one of these stages.

At Chiat/Day we were pretty successful in winning new business. We were able to put together good teams of people who could work on existing business during the day, then devote their nights and weekends to creating new business presentations.

In my last two years at Chiat/Day, I figured that since we were doing the advertising for all of the Nissan dealers around the country, we could do this kind of retail advertising for other clients. I created a separate retail agency within the Chiat/Day Brand Agency called "The

Persuasion Group" where I learned a lot about the nature of these four stages of new business.

Because we were part of Chiat/Day we could generally get invited to participate in reviews, and we always did well in the credentials stage, usually making it into the final pitch. But we never won. In retrospect, I realize that we did not have a compelling message. The Persuasion Group was the "below the radar" part of Chiat/Day, not the famous part. We hadn't won any awards. We didn't have the Energizer Bunny or Air Jordan commercials to show. All that was listed on our resume were commercials that featured the latest incentive offers for Nissan dealers.

Because of my background in pitching for new business, whenever I sit down with my SCORE clients I encourage them to really think through the new business process. Where are they weak? Where are they strong? What is their conversion rate at each stage of this process?

Getting new service-oriented business is really about winning. Like football, basketball, and other sports, you have to have a good team that can come up with a victory. It is not enough just to compete. You must win. And to win consistently you need to understand what you have to do to score points. You must know how to win at each stage in the new business process.

## SUMMARY

So, now you know about the two growth strategies: 1) Get More Money from Existing Customers, and 2) Get More New Customers.

Obviously, in your business you will need to utilize both of these strategies. However, the key is to find the proper balance. Some very successful businesses spend

80% of their effort and marketing on Strategy #1, Getting More Money from Existing Customers. Other successful businesses concentrate the majority of their marketing efforts on Strategy #2, Getting More New Customers.

Whatever the ratio, it's really up to you. In the beginning, getting more money from existing customers makes more sense because it's clearly a less expensive route. The other advantage of this strategy is that it's a great place for you to utilize the marketing tools of social media, which we addressed in Chapter 4.

| EXAMPLES OF GET MORE $ FROM EXISTING CUSTOMERS |
| --- |
| **APPLE** |
| *iPod* <br> *iTunes* <br> *Apps* |
| **CHIAT/DAY** |
| *Got Nissan National Account* <br> *Added Nissan Dealer Account* <br> *Added Nissan Infiniti Account* <br> *Added Nissan International Account* |
| **ARM & HAMMER BAKING SODA** |
| *Encouraged Customers to* <br> *Change Box Every Three Months* |

## EXAMPLES OF GET MORE NEW CUSTOMERS

### APPLE

*New Products*
*New Distribution (Retail Stores)*
*New Packaging*
*Better Value*

### NIKE

*New Categories: Track Shoes, Running Shoes,*
*Basketball Shoes, Apparel, Golf/NFL*

### CHIAT/DAY

*Understand New Business Process:*
*Win Competition: Nissan, Nike, Pizza Hut*

### SCORE

*New Variety of Seminars:*
*Events, Women's Business Conference*

### MCDONALD'S

*Adding Menu Items*

### WOLFGANG PUCK

*New Products: Pizza, Soup, Salads*
*New Distribution: Express Restaurants (Airports)*

# THE IMPORTANCE OF YOU

## Chapter 13

# THE IMPORTANCE OF YOU

Now that you have learned all about "The Big 5" marketing strategies that can help you grow your business, there is just one other extremely important component of achieving success with my *Marketing Without Money* concept: YOU.

In a small business (and sometimes even larger businesses), the single most important difference between success and failure is the leadership of the company, the person in charge.

Apple is a perfect example. It's obvious that Steve Jobs was a brilliant leader and a very successful business person. However, in my opinion, a lot of other people could have created the same successful products like the iPod, the iPhone, and the iPad, etc.

I truly believe that Job's greatest achievement and the thing that sets him apart from other mere mortals was his ability to create iTunes. This was no easy task. Think about it. He had to convince the record companies that their paradigm of selling 10 to 13-song albums or discs was not the best packaging. He persuaded some of the smartest and most egotistical people in the world into believing that he had a better way.

The fact that he was able to pull this off still amazes me. This is testimony to the person that Steve Jobs was, not the company called Apple.

When Jobs left in 1985, Apple still had all of the technology and resources to succeed. What they lost, however, was a leader with a compelling vision to organize and orchestrate these resources into a successful business enterprise. Without him at the helm, Apple floundered and almost became extinct.

As the owner of a business, you are the captain of your ship. You must determine your destination and navigate a course to reach your goal.

During my 10 years as a SCORE counselor, I have met face-to-face with more than a thousand small-business owners and entrepreneurs just like you. During that time I have had the privilege to help some of these people achieve incredible success, while others never seem to find their way. What is the difference between those who become successful and those who do not?

Like most things in life, the answer is complicated. But in my opinion, one of the biggest single factors that separates successful business owners from the less successful is their clarity of purpose combined with a passionate intensity to make something better for consumers. They want to sell and/or distribute products or services that will make people look better, feel better, or do better by performing some activity at a higher level.

When I sit down with my SCORE clients at the Starbucks in Dana Point, I tell them I am not interested in looking at blueprints, patents, or their business plan. I want to learn about them; who they are, what they know, what they want, and why they are in business. What is their purpose?

If someone tells me they are interested in starting a business because they want to make a lot of money, I generally suggest that I am probably not the right counselor for them. It's not that I am against people making a lot of money. But I believe that financial reward is a consequence of something else. In business, if you successfully figure out how to serve the wants and needs of your targeted prospects and you do this better than your competition, you can make a lot of money. Steve Jobs and Phil Knight are perfect examples of this tactic.

The reality is that there are easier and less demanding ways to earn money than by starting up a business. We all know the grim statistics; more than 75% of all new businesses fail in the first two years.

On the positive side, I have been blessed to work with several SCORE clients who have achieved great success. (See "Success Stories" Chapter 15.)

Giselle Chapman was one of those people. When I first met Giselle in 2008, she was selling PowerPoint presentations to mid-level managers for around $3,000. I helped Giselle focus her business on a new and more specific target audience: CEOs who cared about their communications and the culture of their business. Today, five years later, Giselle markets herself as a "Performance Optimizer" and sells six-month Team Building/Culture Transformation programs. She ignites passion and performance in CEOs of $50 million businesses across the country, and instead of selling PowerPoint presentations, she now charges $40,000 for her training programs.

Giselle's success did not come about because she created a new product or redesigned her web page. It was because she gained a new perspective. She realized that clients weren't buying her "stuff," they were buying her. They were attracted to her dynamic personality, her unbridled enthusiasm and energy. They were buying her in hopes that her motivation and vision would spark a new commitment and greater energy, in other words, a new culture in their employees.

Giselle's story is incredibly relevant for everyone who is in a service business, where in many cases, the customer is buying a "person" or a "group of people" that the client perceives as valuable.

When I was at Chiat/Day, clients hired the agency, but frequently what they wanted to buy was our Creative Director, Lee Clow, because of his passion and his unbounded enthusiasm and conviction. When we made our final new business presentation to the executives of Pizza Hut, its President, Art Gunther, said to Lee, "I don't really know what you said, but you said it with such conviction and passion that I want you to do that for our company." Then Gunther hired our agency to handle the national advertising for Pizza Hut.

We can see additional examples of how important the person is to product businesses—not just with Steve Jobs—but Howard Schultz at Starbucks, Jeff Bezos at Amazon, Tony Hsieh at Zappos, and many others.

Of course, my main reason for writing this book was to try to help you grow your business. But a secondary goal was to help you remember why you wanted to start your business in the first place. You wanted to be your own boss, you wanted to solve a problem, or you wanted more people to have access to your products.

One of my objectives when I counsel people is to get them re-energized about their business. I try to be a cheerleader and a coach. I want to let them know that there is a team of experienced and knowledgeable people at SCORE who are eager to help them succeed.

Dealing with actual small-business owners who are struggling with very limited resources and money, has reminded me that marketing isn't some theoretical, abstract subject. Marketing is alive and pulsating in the hearts and minds of all of those small-business owners. It's the blood coursing through their veins.

Marketing is driven and sustained by one thing that doesn't cost a dime: ideas about how you can make your products or services perform better for your customers; how you can make them more attractive, accessible, and valuable to the consumer. Ideas are the wind in your sails, the fuel in your tank. Ideas are the energy that propels your business on its journey toward success.

At the core, marketing is about you and your ideas. It is about how you transform your dreams into a reality, determine your destination, and reach your goal.

Hopefully, I have helped you to understand what *Marketing Without Money* is and how you can utilize these ideas to grow your business. As your business begins to increase, be sure to take advantage of the terrific resources available from SCORE; go to the many seminars, workshops and conferences and take advantage of the FREE personal mentoring and counseling services.

Most important, have confidence in yourself. Believe that you can do it! If you have the passion and the determination required to start a business, combined with the willingness to seek help when you need it, there is no doubt in my mind that you can achieve success.

# SUMMARY/CONCLUSION

## Chapter 14

# SUMMARY/CONCLUSION

This is the part of the book where I am going to explain to you in a nutshell, everything I have tried to teach you in *Marketing Without Money*.

I believe that "The Big 5" marketing strategies that follow will help you grow your business more than anything else:

- **Strategy #1:** Solve More Consumer Needs or Wants (Product)

**How to Implement This Strategy:** Create new products or services.

- **Strategy #2:** Make Your Product, Service, or Business More Attractive (Packaging)

**How to Implement This Strategy:** Think of how you can improve the aesthetic appearance of everything that customers or clients see about your business.

- **Strategy #3:** Make it Easier/More Convenient for the Consumer to Buy Your Product or Service (Distribution)

**How to Implement This Strategy:** Expand your distribution using the Internet, or in the real world, open more stores, service centers, or offices.

• **Strategy #4:** Increase Your Value Equation (Value)

**How to Implement This Strategy:** Be more valuable to your customers or clients by adding more benefits.

• **Strategy #5:** Be Better Known (Promotion)

**How to Implement This Strategy:** Increase awareness to your target audience. Move your customers down the Purchase Funnel: Awareness, Consideration, Shopping, Intention, Buy, and Love. Be clear about what you want to be known for.

In conjunction with "The Big 5" marketing strategies, I recommend that you also implement the following specific tactics or ideas.

• **Identify & Select the Right Target Prospect:** Target the person who is most likely to purchase your products or services. Focus all of your efforts and resources on this defined target.

• **All Customers Are Not Equal:** There are four types of customers, from the highly valuable Evangelist to the Good, the Bad, and the Ugly. Your job is to get more Evangelists and Good customers to grow your business and reduce or eliminate the Bad and the Ugly.

• **Promote One Benefit:** Be known for something to someone, rather than everything to everybody. Select one benefit that you can consistently promote.

• **Define Your Growth Strategy:** There are only two ways to grow your business; 1) Get more money from existing customers, and 2) Get more new customers. What percentage of your time and resources are you devoting to each of these activities?

In this book I have tried to simplify the job of marketing into something you can do and understand. Remember, I believe that you have been marketing all of your life. Whenever you've tried to attract someone or something, you were marketing.

In the end, marketing is simply the behavior associated with recognizing and trying to solve someone else's needs, wants, or desires.

As the owner and operator of a small business, you may not have much of a marketing budget, but if you use your brain and allow yourself to be creative by substituting ideas for money, you can be very successful. You can have fun and grow your business by *Marketing Without Money*.

# SCORE SUCCESS STORIES

# Chapter 15

# SCORE SUCCESS STORIES

### TASHA OLDHAM, My Story, Inc.
### www.mystoryinc.com

Tasha spent 15 years as a documentary filmmaker. Then one day she decided that she wanted to have her own company, so she went into business for herself and created My Story, Inc. With the help of the SCORE National Foundation, Tasha has grown her business by filming videos for clients like Deluxe Corporation, First Team Real Estate and other major companies.

### JONI MARIE O'NEILL, Mission Viejo Florist
### www.missionviejoflorist.com

Joni was a nurse in the emergency room of a hospital before she found a flower shop she wanted to buy in 1997. It wasn't until afterwards that she learned about SCORE and attended several seminars, taking advantage of the free counseling.

In the past four years, the number of florists in Mission Viejo diminished from eight to four stores. But during this same time, Joni's business has flourished. By 2010 Joni had grown her business to more than a million dollars in annual revenue.

## PAZIT BEN EZRI, LulyBoo LLC
## www.lulyboo.com

Pazit is a wife and mother of three children who started a business to solve a problem. Her infant son wasn't comfortable and couldn't sleep whenever they traveled away from home. Pazit decided to take matters into her own hands. She bought a sewing machine and learned how to sew, then made her first LulyBoo lounge, a soft bassinet that can be folded up and carried as a backpack.

Her child was finally happy when they left the house, and could fall asleep anywhere. Afterwards, other mothers came up to her and asked her where she got this great product. Pazit decided there was a consumer demand and created LulyBoo LLC. With the help of her SCORE Counselor, Bob Godlasky, she has distribution in Babies"R"Us, Target, Bergstroms, and many other locations. LulyBoo sales have tripled in Babies"R"Us and now, other important retailers like SkyMall and Diapers.com are calling.

## YOUNGSONG MARTIN, Wildflower Linens
## www.wildflowerlinens.com

Born in South Korea, Youngsong came to the U.S. when she was in her twenties, starting her career as a fashion designer. One day she said, "I have to live my dream and not pursue somebody else's." Combining her love for entertaining and fine dining with her expert knowledge of textiles and fabrics, she created a new company in the décor rental business called, "Wildflower Linen."

With the help of SCORE Counselors, Terri Carr and Jim Anderson, her business revenues tripled. Today, Wildflower Linen is the leading designer and producer of specialty table linens and chair covers for events. She has decorated rooms for post-Oscar parties, the Grammy's, and even the White House. Her clients include many major Hollywood celebrities and Fortune 500 companies.

## GISELLE CHAPMAN
www.gisellechapman.com

Giselle Chapman started out selling PowerPoint presentations to mid-level executives for $3,000. Now, she's selling intensive team building sessions to Fortune 500 companies for $40,000. Giselle has grown her business by following a simple growth strategy: get more money out of your existing clients. She did this by building relationships with her clients, who appreciate that she is not trying to sell them something. Instead, she is trying to help them create a better, more effective organization. Giselle always exceeds her clients' expectations.

## ROY & LOUISE VAN BROEKHUIZEN, Laga Bags
www.laga-handbags.com

When Roy van Broekhuizen was sent to Indonesia in 2004 to help the tsunami victims, he came across some survivors who were creating beautiful woven bags. With the help of his wife, Louise, they started Laga Bags, importing and selling the bags around the world. A percentage of the profits are then returned to the women who make the bags, manifesting the concept that it is better to teach a man to fish than to give him a fish. Working with SCORE, Laga Bags has revenues in excess of $1 million.

## YOU!

You just may be the next SCORE success story.

# CASE STUDIES:

*How Nike and Apple Grew Their Businesses*

# Chapter 16

# CASE STUDIES:

## *How Nike and Apple Grew Their Businesses*

A lot of small-business owners want to emulate the great success of Apple, Nike and other super growth companies. But generally they forget that in the beginning, Apple and Nike were just like them, a small company with no employees and no money.

I advise my clients, "Don't try to copy the marketing activities of the $19 billion Nike business or Apple's Mega-World. Instead, focus more on Phil Knight selling track shoes out of the back of his car at track meets or the Apple marketing activities that began in Steve Job's parents' garage."

To give you a glimpse of how long it took these two mega-companies to achieve the success they are hailed for today, let's take a look at the evolution of their growth.

**NIKE: "There is No Finish Line"**

Phil Knight started what became known as Nike in 1964 when he traveled around to track meets peddling his shoes. He knew how to find his target audience—people who need and buy track shoes—at high school and college track meets. This was long before Nike had a multi-million dollar marketing budget, prior to the swoosh logo, and way before Phil Knight became a billionaire.

In every great business success story, in addition to hard work and skill, there is always a considerable amount of luck or good fortune. In Phil Knight's case, he was fortunate to be in the right place at exactly the right time.

In 1974, Phil Knight introduced a new product that Bill Bowerman invented using his wife's waffle iron—and without permission as the story goes. Called the Waffle Trainer, this new type of running shoe provided better cushioning for long distance running on streets and pavement, better than anything else on the market.

A few years before this invention the only people running on city streets were young kids or criminals trying to escape the police. In the 1950s the percentage of adults running for fitness was probably less than 1%. Knight and Bowerman just happened to develop this new product at the same time that there was an emerging market for recreational runners called "Baby Boomers."

Then a guy named Jim Fixx wrote a bestselling book, *The Complete Book of Running*, promoting a health advantage of long distance running. Almost overnight, ordinary people started hitting the streets. Soon there were 10k races and half marathons and even full 26-mile marathons that were attracting hundreds of thousands of people who needed running shoes, coinciding with the maturing of the Baby Boomers.

By definition, "Baby Boomers" are the 76 million people who were born between 1946 and 1972. I was born in 1945, so all of my life I have been the nose of the Baby Boomer Generation. I saw what was happening first.

At every stage I've watched a phenomenon occur, where whatever I was interested in, millions of other people were hooked on as well. First it was rock and roll,

Elvis, the Beatles, transcendental meditation, yoga, and long distance running.

Phil Knight was at the intersection of a new idea (long distance running) and a product (the Waffle Trainer), along with the emergence of a new market of buyers, the Baby Boomers who had the time, the money, and the desire to be healthy and fit. Bingo, the running market was created.

There are generally three essential components that come together to create a new market:

1. A new idea (Running is good for you)

2. A consumer base (76 million Baby Boomers)

3. A new technology (The Waffle Trainer running shoe)

In marketing, good timing may not be everything, but it's right up there with whatever is in second place. If Bowerman had invented the Waffle Trainer in 1945, there would've been no market for this product.

Similarly, if Bill Gates and Steve Jobs were born 20 years earlier they wouldn't have been able to create huge businesses in the personal computer market. That's because computer chips did not exist. The idea that everyone needs a computer was non-existent. There were no consumers remotely interested in such a product. Only big corporations and government agencies owned computers, not individuals.

Now, let's take a closer look at how Phil Knight grew Nike from nothing to a $19 billion business in the timeline on the following page.

| NIKE TIMELINE | |
|---|---|
| 1964 | Phil Knight & Bill Bowerman create Blue Ribbon Sports. Phil Knight sells Tiger Track Shoes out of the back of his car at track meets. |
| 1969 | Blue Ribbon sales reach $1 million. Phil Knight quits his job teaching. |
| 1971 | Nike Brand Name & Swoosh logo created |
| 1972 | Waffle Trainer Shoes created, shoes that runners want. Sales reach $3.5 million. |
| 1973 | Nike signs first professional athlete tennis star, Ilie Nastase to endorsement deal. |
| 1980 | Nike becomes public company |
| 1984 | Nike hires Chiat/Day, introduces apparel line, as well as Air Jordan shoe, that dominates 1984 Olympics |
| 1986 | Nike fires Chiat/Day and returns to Weiden & Kennedy Advertising |
| 2011 | Nike has revenues of $19 Billion |

Hopefully, you are beginning to get the picture here. Growing a business is about anticipating and responding to emerging marketing opportunities, combined with the good fortune of being at the right place at the right time. It took Nike 47 years to become the $19 billion company we know today. Remember, it all began with Phil Knight selling shoes out of his car at track meets.

## APPLE: "I Want to Change the World"

As every American who can read knows, Steve Jobs started his business with Steve Wozniak in his parents' garage in 1976. The Steve Jobs story has many similarities with Phil Knight's. In the beginning, Steve Jobs did not have a multi-million dollar marketing budget nor did he have a famous logo or a Gulf Stream private jet.

Also, like the Nike story, three events occurred to create a new growth market:

1. A new idea was conceived that everyone needs a personal computer. At the time, this was very

outrageous. The thought that someone other than a giant company (an individual) would actually buy a computer, was totally ridiculous. Similar to many original great ideas, it was scoffed at by many.

2. Technology evolved. The invention of the silicon microchip made it possible to construct a computing machine that was both smaller and more powerful than the giant main frame computers that dominated the business world.

3. A new market was created by new software such as Microsoft Excel and Word that gave consumers the ability to create and manipulate financial statements and word documents with much greater ease.

Job's and Wozniak's first really successful product was the Apple II, introduced in 1977. Chiat/Day was hired by Apple to create their advertising a year later because Jay Chiat knew Regis McKinna, the owner of the public relations firm for Apple. A few years later Chiat/Day bought the Regis McKinna agency and incorporated it into their agency services.

Back in 1983, Chiat/Day proposed the outrageous idea that Apple should introduce its newest computer, the Macintosh, by running a commercial during the 1984 Super Bowl.

This was truly a phenomenal idea because at this time there really was NOT a large market for personal computers. The PC market, as we now know it, was just in its infancy. IBM had recently thrown its hat in the ring with its own model, which added credibility to the notion that there really was (or would be) a large market for personal computers.

From one point of view, spending millions of dollars on a television commercial for a personal computer was a totally ridiculous idea. But from another, it was brilliant. If you could create a truly unique and interesting commercial that got everyone talking, you might be able to stimulate the market and actually help it grow. It was also a brilliant way to pit the Apple computer against its main competitors, Microsoft and IBM, who catered to engineers, accountants, and computer programmers.

The 1984 television commercial was all about positioning Apple as the computer for the rest of us. To see the commercial, go to www.YouTube.com and type in "1984 Apple's Macintosh Commercial."

Prior to 1984, people who bought computers were pretty much geeks. Why, because in order to use a computer you basically had to be a computer programmer or a genius. Computers, to say the least, were NOT user-friendly. The Macintosh was a different kind of personal computer, though. It had a mouse that made it easy to operate. No more keystrokes to command the computer. It looked friendly and allowed the user to create graphics, not just words.

And so, the "1984" commercial ran, millions of people saw it, and talked about it the next day at the office around the water cooler. Apple was off and running and the rest is, as they say, history.

Apple was able to grow its business from 1983 to more than $300 billion in 2011. Notice in the following timeline that the growth of Apple came from a brilliant combination of new products, new distribution (retail stores), and new promotion ("Think Different"). If these ideas sound familiar, it is because they are some of "The Big 5" marketing strategies.

| APPLE TIMELINE | |
|---|---|
| 1976 | Jobs & Wozniak sign partnership agreement, set up shop in Job's parents' garage. |
| 1977 | Apple Computer, a new corporation officially created. Value=$5,309. Apple II launched, sells 2,500 units |
| 1980 | Apple goes public on December 12, 1980 at $2.75 per share on the NYSE. Today its stock price equals $532.17 per share. |
| 1981 | Apple hires Chiat/Day |
| 1983 | Steve Jobs hires John Scully as CEO |
| 1984 | Introduction of the most famous TV Macintosh commercial in 1984, on Super Bowl XVIII |
| 1985-86 | Jobs leaves Apple. Chiat/Day fired as ad agency. |
| 1997 | January: Jobs returns to Apple as part-time advisor. July: Apple re-hires Chiat/Day. "Think Different" ad debuts. |
| 1998 | iMac introduced |
| 2001 | January: iTunes introduced. May: First Apple Store. October: iPod introduced |
| 2007 | iPhone introduced |
| 2010 | iPad introduced |
| 2011 | Apple revenue = $300 billion |

You might be wondering what the point is of all this history. Well, it's to remind you that "overnight success" takes years. These two multi-billion-dollar companies began with very little money, few resources, a handful of employees, and just one or two products. But what they lacked in money and resources, they more than made up for with ideas.

Both Phil Knight and Steve Jobs had a vision. They had a clarity of purpose. They knew who their target was and they did not try to be something for everyone.

Nike's core philosophy was about athletic performance. They wanted to sell products to athletes to help them win. Apple's philosophy was about creating technology that regular people (not computer specialists) could use. Their primary focus was to come up with a computer that was easy to use for the average person. Long before there was a market for desktop computers, Steve Jobs and Steve Wozniak envisioned this world.

I'm sure that someday, someone else will reach the pinnacle of success like Steve Jobs or Phil Knight. Odds are, it could even be someone reading this book. It is totally possible, you know. Just don't expect it to happen overnight.

# ACKNOWLEDGEMENTS

## CAREER MENTORS

## ADVERTISING

Jay Chiat, Founder and CEO of Chiat/Day Advertising Agency, hired me in 1977 and gave me a chance to "see how big we could get without becoming bad" in the advertising agency industry.

Lee Clow, friend and colleague with whom I worked for 21 years at Chiat/Day showed me what the words "Good Enough is Not Enough" really meant.

Bill Tragos, Founder and CEO of TBWA Advertising became my boss and good friend in 1996 when Chiat/Day was purchased by Omnicom and merged with TBWA Advertising.

## SCORE

Bill Morland, past chairman of SCORE 114, helped me through the "provisional phase" of becoming a SCORE volunteer and helped me find my "place" within the SCORE organization where I could make a contribution.

Ed Reardon created relationships with local libraries that allowed SCORE 114 to begin developing and presenting workshops and seminars.

Mark Dobosz, President of the SCORE Foundation, helped direct all of my net proceeds from the sale of this book to be donated to the SCORE Foundation.

Jerome Chiaro, SCORE colleague, helped me understand social media.

Martin Edwards, SCORE colleague, helped generate thousands of emails to promote my marketing seminars.

Carl LeKander, SCORE colleague, helps me make sure I have everything I need to present at my seminars.

All of the more than 100 terrific volunteers at SCORE 114, Orange County Chapter, who spend their time helping SCORE clients to grow their businesses.

## CHIAT/DAY CLIENTS

## YAMAHA MOTORCYCLES, USA

John Rinek, as Advertising Manager for Yamaha Motorcycles, USA, was my first client in 1977 and has continued to be my friend for the past 35 years. Later, John became my client at Nissan Motors, USA, where he was Director of Advertising.

Dennis Stefani, Marketing Director for Yamaha Motorcycles, USA, first introduced me to the concept of the Purchase Process and the wisdom of Peter Drucker. (Dennis is most famous for being the father of Gwen Stefani of "No Doubt" fame.)

## PIZZA HUT

Art Gunther, President of Pizza Hut in 1983, hired Chiat/Day and gave us a chance to do great work for a national brand.

Steve Reinemund, President of Pizza Hut in 1985-86, helped me learn about the pizza business and allowed me to participate in the development of their delivery business. Steve later went on to become CEO of PepsiCo Worldwide.

## NIKE, INC.

Rob Strasser and Peter Moore, Marketing and Creative Directors, hired Chiat/Day in 1983 and, along with CEO, Phil Knight, pushed us to do great work for the 1984 Los Angeles Olympics and the Air Jordan Campaign.

## NISSAN MOTORS, USA

Tom Mignanelli, President & CEO of Nissan Motors, USA (1987-93), hired Chiat/Day as its advertising agency for the Nissan brand and later gave us the Nissan dealer business and the Infiniti account.

Bob Thomas, President & CEO of Nissan Motors, USA (1993-97), encouraged Chiat/Day to create some of the best advertising in the automotive industry, including the famous "Barbie & GI Joe" television commercial for the 300ZX.

## APPLE, INC.

Steve Jobs, who, although I never worked with him directly and had only a few conversations, helped put Chiat/Day on the map with the famous "1984" TV commercial to introduce the Macintosh Computer.

## MY TEAM AT CHIAT/DAY

Thanks to my Team: Steve Goldman, Pam Keehn, Mark Bilfield, Monty Zator, and Kristen McCoy, without whom I never could have achieved anything at Chiat/Day Advertising.

# MY "MARKETING WITHOUT MONEY" SUPPORT TEAM

Wendell & Nancy Chong: Click Business Strategies, my tech team, handles my Facebook Page and helps create graphics for my seminars.

Bill Taylor: My videographer for my *Marketing Without Money* YouTube Videos, friend, and sailing partner.

John Rinek: Retired Marketing Executive, who agreed to read my manuscript pre-publication and offered valuable advice.

Susan Rinek: My longtime friend who designed the terrific book cover for *Marketing Without Money*; a great job of making the packaging more attractive.

Kathy Moore: My proofreader

Donna Jost: My valuable co-writer, editor, and publisher at Endless Dreams Publishing

## PERSONAL

My Wife, Susan: Special thanks to my wonderful wife for putting up with me for the past 17 years. Susan has always encouraged me in all of my creative interests.

## MY SCORE CLIENTS

Thanks to all of the great small-business owners and entrepreneurs who have attended my marketing seminars and one-on-one counseling sessions. You are my inspiration and my "why!"

# BIBLIOGRAPHY

## SOCIAL MEDIA

A Report by Harvard Business Review Analytic Services, "The New Conversation: Taking Social Media from Talk to Action," *Harvard Business Review*, August 2010

Carroll, David, "United Breaks Guitars: The Power of One Voice in the Age of Social Media," May 15, 2012, Hay House

Jackson, John Bradley, "DeJa New Marketing: Increase Sales with Social Media, Search Marketing, Email Marketing, Blogs, and More," June 30, 2012, Dog Ear Publishing

Rogers, David L., "The Network is Your Customer: 5 Strategies to Thrive in the Digital Age," November 13, 2012, Yale University Press

Saylor, Michael, "The Mobile Wave: How Mobile Intelligence Will Change Everything," June 26, 2012, Vanguard Press

Solis, Brian, "The End of Business as Usual: Rewire the Way You Work to Succeed in the Consumer Revolution," October 18, 2011, Wiley

## GENERAL BUSINESS BOOKS

Auletta, Ken, "Googled: The End of the World as We Know It," October 26, 2010, Penguin Books

Byrne, John A., "World Changers: 25 Entrepreneurs Who Changed Business As We Knew It," December 8, 2011, Portfolio Hardcover

Drucker, Peter F., and Synnestvedt, Erik, "The Five Most Important Questions You Will Ever Ask About Your Organization," October 30, 2008, Gildan Media

Drucker, Peter F., and Wartzman, Rick, "The Drucker Lectures: Essential Lessons on Management, Society, and Economy," June 14, 2010, McGraw-Hill

Drucker, Peter F., "Innovation and Entrepreneurship," May 9, 2006, Harper Business

Drucker, Peter F., "The Practice of Management," October 3, 2006, Harper Business

Gerber, Michael E. "The E Myth Revisited: Why Most Small Businesses Don't Work and What To Do About It," March 3, 1995, Harper Collins

Haidt, Jonathan, "The Righteous Mind: Why Good People are Divided by Politics and Religion," May 28, 2013, Your Coach In A Box

Hsieh, Tony, and Rob Ten Pas, "Delivering Happiness: A Path to Profits, Passion, and Purpose; A Round Table Comic," April 16, 2012, Writers of the Round Table Press

Isaacson, Walter, "Steve Jobs," October 24, 2011, Simon & Schuster

Robinson, Ken, and Aronica, Lou, "The Element: How Finding Your Passion Changes Everything," December 29, 2009, Penguin Books

Sinek, Simon, "Start With Why: How Great Leaders Inspire Everyone to Take Action," December 27, 2011, Portfolio Trade

Zane, Chris, "Reinventing the Wheel: The Science of Creating Lifetime Customers," March 8 2011, BenBella Books

## MARKETING BOOKS

Decker, Bert, "You've Got to Be Believed to Be Heard," 2008, St. Martin's Press

Godin, Seth, "Purple Cow: Transform Your Business by Being Remarkable," July 1, 2007, Penguin Books

Kawasaki, Guy, "Enchantment: The Art of Changing Hearts, Minds, and Actions," December 31, 2012, Portfolio Trade

Levitt, Theodore, "Ted Levitt on Marketing," July 1, 2006, Harvard Business Press

Levitt, Theodore, "The Marketing Imagination," October 1, 1983, The Free Press

Ogilvy, David, & Parker, Sir Alan, "Confessions of an Advertising Man," January 1, 2012, Southbank Publishing

Ogilvy, David, "Ogilvy on Advertising," March 12, 1985, Vintage

Ries, Al, "Focus: The Future of Your Company Depends On It," September 27, 2005, Harper Business

Ries, Al, Trout, Jack, and Kotler, Philip, "Positioning: The Battle for Your Mind," December 13, 2000, McGraw-Hill

Ries, Al, and Trout, Jack, "The 22 Immutable Laws of Marketing: Violate Them At Your Own Risk!" April 27, 1994, Harper Business

Ries, Al, and Trout, Jack, "Marketing Warfare," 1987, Mass Paperback

Stabiner, Karen, "Inventing Desire: Inside Chiat/Day: The Hottest Shop, the Coolest Players, the Big Business of Advertising," May 1993, Simon & Schuster

# TOM PATTY'S
# MARKETING WITHOUT MONEY

## CONTACT INFORMATION

### Website:
http://www.TomPattysMarketingWithoutMoney.com

### Facebook:
http://www.facebook.com/
tompattysmarketingwithoutmoney

### Twitter:
http://www.twitter.com/tompattytweets

### SCORE Orange County:
http://www.score114.org

### SCORE National:
http://www.score.org

**NOTES:** _____

_____

_____

_____

_____

_____

_____

_____

_____

_____

_____

_____

_____

_____

_____

_____

_____

**NOTES:** _____

_____

_____

_____

_____

_____

_____

_____

_____

_____

_____

_____

_____

_____

_____

_____

_____

**NOTES:** _____

_____

_____

_____

_____

_____

_____

_____

_____

_____

_____

_____

_____

_____

_____

_____

_____

**NOTES:** _____

_____

_____

_____

_____

_____

_____

_____

_____

_____

_____

_____

_____

_____

_____

_____